Three Minutes a Day

VOLUME 51

THREE MINUTES A DAY
VOLUME 51

Tony Rossi
Editor-in-Chief

Gerald M. Costello
Contributing Editor

The Christophers
5 Hanover Square
New York, NY 10004

www.christophers.org

Lord, make me an instrument of Your peace.
Where there is hatred, let me sow love;
where there is injury, pardon;
where there is doubt, faith;
where there is despair, hope;
where there is darkness, light;
and where there is sadness, joy.

O Divine Master, grant that I may not so much seek
to be consoled as to console;
to be understood as to understand;
to be loved as to love.
For it is in giving that we receive;
it is in pardoning that we are pardoned;
and it is in dying that we are born to eternal life.
Amen.

PRAYER OF ST. FRANCIS
(ADOPTED AS THE PRAYER OF THE CHRISTOPHERS)

The Christophers warmly thank
all our friends, sponsors and supporters
who have made this 51st volume of
Three Minutes a Day possible.

Contributing Writers

Tony Rossi

Gerald M. Costello

Sarah E. Holinski

Joan Bromfield

Garan Santicola

Joanne K. McPortland

Dear Friend,

We present Volume 51 of our "Three Minutes a Day" book with the hope that it will enliven your heart and lift your spirits throughout the year. One short reading each day can do that when it contains truths that point to the beauty of God's love for us all. We invite you to share these stories with friends and loved ones and request extra copies of this book to pass along to anyone open to The Christophers' uplifting message.

"Three Minutes a Day" is a beloved classic, made possible through the generosity of our donors, who understand the power of hope to transform people's lives. The Christophers are privileged to learn of such transformations through the regular communications we have with those on the front lines of some of the toughest ministries.

One of the people expressing gratitude for our donation of Christopher materials was Deacon Peter Andre, Director of Prison Ministry for the Diocese of St. Petersburg, Florida. He wrote: "Over the years, our volunteers have shared with us what the generosity of your gifts mean to the men and women at the prisons! Even a small item, such as a prayer card, can make a great difference in their lives."

We extend this gratitude expressed by Deacon Peter to all who support our mission. It is only with your help that we are able to continue lighting candles in the darkness. Thank you!

Mary Ellen Robinson, Vice President
Father Jonathan Morris
Father Dennis W. Cleary, M.M.

A Prayer to Welcome the New Year

The inspirational newsletter *Apple Seeds* featured the following prayer for the new year, written by an unknown author:

"Come, Holy Spirit, Spirit of the Risen Christ, be with us today and always. Be our Light, our Guide, and our Comforter. Be our Strength, our Courage, and our Sanctifier.

"May this new year be a time of deep spiritual growth for us, a time of welcoming Your graces and gifts, a time for forgiving freely and unconditionally, a time for growing in virtue and goodness.

"Come, Holy Spirit, be with us today and always. Amen."

Do not remember the former things, or consider the things of old. I am about to do a new thing; now it springs forth, do you not perceive it? I will make a way in the wilderness and rivers in the desert. (Isaiah 43:18-19)

As we embark on the adventure of a new year together, Lord, help me to grow in love for others—and guide me toward becoming more like You.

You're Never Too Old for a Family

"Do you know what it's like to know [that] if I die tomorrow, I don't belong to anyone," said college student Brittany Bullock to her professor, Lorine Ogurkis.

Brittany had lived in five different foster homes since age nine. When she turned 18, her foster parents left her in a Wilkes-Barre, Pennsylvania park, with all her possessions in garbage bags.

The teen stayed with friends, but decided to share her story with Ogurkis after the professor revealed to her class that she and her husband had adopted a baby boy several years ago. As reported by CitizensVoice.com, Ogurkis felt heartbroken at Brittany's plight and vowed that she would never be alone again.

They began going out for meals together and soon, the Ogurkis family invited Brittany to live with them. Even better, in 2016, they adopted her, officially making her Brittany Ogurkis. Brittany said, "People come up to me and say, 'You're 21, aren't you an adult?' Yes, I am an adult. But I still deserve a family."

It is not the children of the flesh who are the children of God, but the children of the promise are counted as descendants. (Romans 9:8)

Lead foster children to their forever families, Father.

A 911 Hunger Emergency

As a 911 operator in Fayetteville, North Carolina, Marilyn Hinson was used to getting all kinds of pleas for help. But her call from 81-year-old prostate cancer survivor Clarence Blackmon was different than most.

As reported by Beth Dreher in *Reader's Digest,* Blackmon, a widower, returned home to an empty refrigerator and pantry after months in the hospital. Unable to get out of the house himself—and with no one in the area to go shopping for him—he dialed 911 and asked if someone could bring him food because he couldn't get out of his chair.

With permission from her supervisor, Hinson bought Blackmon several bags of groceries and made him a few sandwiches that afternoon. She told a local TV station, "I've been hungry. A lot of people can't say that, but I can, and I can't stand for anyone to be hungry."

Blackmon lives in hospice care now, but Hinson still visits him "a few times a week to chat, fill his candy dish, and collect his laundry." He says, "Thank God for people [like Marilyn.]"

The hungry He fills with good things. (Psalm 107:9)

May we always go above and beyond for those in need, Jesus.

The Waze of God

When Father Robert Barron moved to Los Angeles to assume his duties as auxiliary bishop, he downloaded the Waze GPS app to his phone. It provides driving directions and can maneuver you around traffic jams. He thought it was wonderful until the day it prompted him to get off the main highway and take all kinds of slow, local roads to get to his destination.

Angry that he'd followed the Waze app's instructions, he complained about it when he arrived at his meeting. A colleague then told him there had been a tanker spill on the highway that morning, so the app saved him several hours of sitting in traffic.

Bishop Barron saw a lesson in his experience, noting that we often feel lost or disoriented, spiritually speaking. But God calls us to follow His plans, even when they seem counter-intuitive to us.

The bishop concludes, "As we have learned to trust the mechanical voices of our GPS systems in regard to the relatively trivial matter of finding our way past traffic jams, so may we learn to trust the Voice of the one who, as the Psalmist says, 'searches us and knows us and discerns our purpose from afar.'"

With all our heart we follow You. (Daniel 3:41)

Increase my trust in You, Divine Savior.

'We Are All Jews Here'

The future looked bleak for the Jewish American soldiers captured by the Nazis in January 1945 in Ziegenhain, Germany. Though they were already in a POW camp, Jews were systematically singled out and sent to labor camps, where many of them died. U.S. Army Master Sgt. Roddie Edmonds knew that about 200 of his fellow 1,000 soldiers would be in danger if the truth were discovered, so he devised a brave yet risky plan.

As reported by the *Associated Press,* the German camp commander told the Jews to identify themselves. All the camp's inmates stood in front of their barracks. The commander said to Edmonds, "They cannot all be Jews." The Knoxville, Tennessee native responded, "We are all Jews here."

The Nazi put a gun to Edmonds' head and threatened to kill him if he didn't tell the truth. The American responded, "If you are going to shoot, you are going to have to shoot all of us because we know who you are and you'll be tried for war crimes when we win this war."

The Nazi relented. All the Americans survived.

Have no fear or dread of them, because it is the Lord your God who goes with you. (Deuteronomy 31:6)

Instill me with moral courage, Father.

Knit One, Prayer Two

One day, 91-year-old Franciscan Sister Alvera O'Grady saw one of her aides, Amanda LaFrance, knitting a hat on a loom and was immediately intrigued.

"I asked her what she [Amanda] was doing and she explained in her free time she made hats for St. Joseph's Hospital," Sister Alvera told *The Catholic Sun's* Pat Shea. "I asked her if she could teach me how to do it too, and she did… A few of the other sisters saw me creating the hats and they wanted to know how to do it, and before long we had a group together."

Before long, these "tight-knit" nuns in Liverpool, New York, were producing hundreds of hats, many of which they chose to donate to various charities, including their mission school of St. Rose of Lima, located in Peru. While it has only been a year since this group's establishment, their organization has flourished, one small stitch, one colorful hat at a time.

"I feel really happy when I am making them," fellow knitter Sister Eleanor Grace, 85, declared. "If we had a tag line for this ministry it would be 'in every stitch, there is a prayer.'"

Whatever your task, put yourselves into it, as done for the Lord. (Colossians 3:23)

Christ, may every act or work we do be rooted in prayer.

Ten Minutes with Mom and Dad

Sarah Hart may be a Grammy-nominated singer-songwriter, but she makes family her top priority, especially when it comes to her two teenage daughters. She and her husband even have a nightly ritual with the girls to make sure the lines of communication stay open.

During a "Christopher Closeup" interview, Hart said, "We call them downstairs and say, 'It's time for 10 minutes with Mom and Dad.' Then we sit down—with no devices, no electronics—and we each get to pick a different topic. It usually turns into 30 or 40 minutes. We carve out time to make sure that we are speaking to one another as a family, looking in each others' faces, laughing, sometimes crying, but just connecting.

"We are a plugged-in world, and I think that most families [have to] be very intentional about carving out family time. It's a way that we show our children and ourselves and our family, 'I love you to the point that I will put down that stupid computer and spend time with you, and focus on you.' It's been a huge boon in our family life."

Train children in the right way, and when old, they will not stray. (Proverbs 22:6)

Strengthen the bonds within my family, Holy Spirit.

'Can't Beat Goodness Into a Person'

In 1996, the KKK held a rally in Ann Arbor, Michigan, that also drew many protesters who didn't want the racist organization in their community. At one point, a white supremacist with an SS emblem found himself amidst the protesters, and a small group of them chased him, knocked him to the ground, and kicked him, while shouting, "Kill the Nazi!"

That's when African-American high school student Keshia Thomas got involved. She threw herself on top of the man to protect him from being hit anymore. Then she told the crowd, "[You] can't beat goodness into a person."

When asked her motivation, Thomas said, "I knew what it was like to be hurt. I wish someone would have stood up for me...Nobody deserves to be hurt, especially not for an idea."

Thomas never received thanks from the man she helped but, months later, his son approached her to express gratitude for what she had done. She hoped that maybe her act of kindness would end the cycle of hatred and violence in that family.

Put away from you all bitterness and wrath and anger. (Ephesians 4:31)

Where there is hatred, let me bring love, Prince of Peace.

Angels of America's Fallen

One tour of duty in the Marine Corps wasn't enough for Joe Lewis, so he served again in the Army and Air National Guard. As his 50th birthday approached, he grew concerned about the children of his fellow servicemen and women who didn't make it home.

Lewis decided to help them by starting Angels of America's Fallen (AOAF), a nonprofit dedicated to supporting the sons and daughters of deceased military service members and first responders by funding their extracurricular activities. As Lewis told Alyssa Brewer of *Family Circle* magazine, "It's about honoring these heroes' loss and validating their sacrifice."

AOAF was founded in 2012 in the Colorado Springs area, where Lewis lives with his family. Now, after many fundraisers, it's expanded to 29 states and helps over 200 youngsters.

"We want the kids to have an outlet," Lewis says. "We encourage them to try new things, whatever their passion is."

The spirit of the Lord God is upon me...He has sent me...to provide for those who mourn in Zion—to give them a garland instead of ashes. (Isaiah 61:1,3)

Bring comfort to those children who've lost a parent to war, Prince of Peace.

Retirement? Forget About It!

It's somewhat rare for people to live to be 100 years old—and rarer still that they're actually still working at that age. Well, Brooklyn's Madeline Scotto served as an exception to the rule. After graduating from St. Ephrem's Elementary School in 1928, she went on to become a math teacher there and was still working as the math bee coach in 2014.

Ironically, most of Scotto's children are themselves retired! So why did she remain active? She told *WCBS* radio, "I think helping others really is what made me able to be the person I am at 100. I never look forward to the day that I'll retire because there will always be something that I can do, I'm sure. When you're helping others, you're helping yourself."

Students past and present appreciate Scotto's talent and dedication. Nancy Bongiovanni said, "She is the best math teacher my daughters ever had. She has touched the lives of thousands of students in the very best way."

Scotto passed away in 2015, but her legacy and example won't soon be forgotten.

Rich experience is the crown of the aged. (Sirach 25:6)

Help us treasure the wisdom of our elders, Lord, and enable them to stay active in sharing their wisdom.

How a Friend Becomes Family

Mikkee Hall, age 38, lives in her best friend's basement, but it's not because she's facing financial hard times.

Hall used to have a job she enjoyed in Washington, D.C., but she felt lonely because the friends she made there always ended up moving away. Writing in the *Washington Post,* she said, "I was missing that deeper sense of connection."

When Hall's best friend Stephanie, her husband and their four kids—to whom Hall is the godmother—decided to move to Denver, they invited her to join them and live in their basement apartment. Hall took them up on their offer, and the change has given her the feeling of connection she wanted.

She wrote, "I get to chat with my best friend when I get home from work, as she makes dinner and chases the children around. We're there for each other's everyday moments of anxiety...I accompany the kids, with their parents, on their first days of school." Hall concludes, "We have become a family."

All of us are in search of those deeper connections. Be sure to nurture the relationships in your life.

A true friend sticks closer than one's nearest kin. (Proverbs 18:24)

Help me to be a welcoming friend, Father.

When You Disagree

"We don't love each other enough," observed Tom Zampino on his Patheos blog in reference to all the arguing he saw going on both in the real world and online over political, religious, and cultural issues.

He said, "So convinced are we of our own *rightness* in all things, that we fail more times than not to even notice *the other*. Instead of taking note of their humanity—as someone, too, created in God's likeness and image—we see, instead, only positions. And it's easier to dismiss positions than persons."

Zampino concludes, "Putting aside our very substantial, and perhaps very legitimate, differences for the moment, the next time that we feel compelled to respond to the person before us with spite, meanness, bullying or out-and-out hatred...we need to understand that whenever we act without love, not only do we mock our own faith, but we also reject the direct command of Christ Himself...In the end, we need to understand and live the message that it's not us against them. Rather, it's about God *with* us—Emmanuel."

You shall love your neighbor as yourself. (Mark 12:31)

May I treat all Your children with dignity, Creator.

'Everything Starts with One Person'

Maryknoll Father James Keller, who began this series of books after founding The Christophers in 1945, was known for some memorable sayings—including The Christophers' motto, "It's better to light one candle than to curse the darkness."

Here are some more of Father Keller's thoughts, as spelled out in his writings:

- "Everything starts with one person. I don't care if you are five or 105—God from all eternity chose you to be where you are, at this time in history, to change the world."

- "There's a lot of things that you can do, but you've got to do what God has asked you to do, and stick to it!"

- "We are all called to be great saints. Don't miss the opportunity."

- "God wants you to be in the world, but so different from the world that you will change it. Get cracking."

- "Faith is what gets you started. Hope is what keeps you going. Love is what brings you to the end."

Build one another up, as indeed you are doing. (1 Thessalonians 5:11)

Show me, Holy Spirit, ways to encourage others today.

Comedian Comes Out of Retirement

Fans of comedian Mark Russell were happy to hear that he came out of retirement at age 83. That's wonderful news for clean family entertainment, for Catholic charitable agencies, and anyone who enjoys a good political laugh—at the expense of Republicans, Democrats, and Independents alike.

Mark Zimmermann, editor of the *Catholic Standard* in the nation's capital, wrote about Russell and captured a few of his patented one-liners in the process.

Russell comes originally from Buffalo, where he graduated from Canisius High School, and he'll jokingly blame his Catholic education for his technical-skill shortcomings. "When I was a kid," he'll say, "the nuns never taught the boys how to type. The only electronic device I know how to use in my house is the toaster. I can upload toast." And the male staff at Canisius? "After the Jesuits, the Marines were anti-climactic."

He also jokes about congressional gridlock, saying that Congress tried to pass a resolution commemorating Cinco de Mayo. The only trouble? "They couldn't agree on the date."

**Our mouth was filled with laughter.
(Psalm 126:2)**

Help me to see the humor in everyday life, Holy Spirit.

Don't Live as a Lone Ranger Christian

When Laura Story was caring for her husband Martin in the aftermath of his brain surgery, she had virtually no time to do anything else, including go to church. That's when she gained a new perspective on what "church" really is.

During a "Christopher Closeup" interview about her book "When God Doesn't Fix It," she said, "Growing up, church was a place that we would go. With Martin in the hospital, we couldn't go to church—but the church came to us. We had people that did everything from bringing us meals to helping sit with Martin through the night so I could get some rest. And people would go to our home and literally clean our toilet.

"It was amazing to see the hands and feet of Jesus coming around and serving us. I think the lesson to be learned is that God never created us to live as Lone Ranger Christians. It's about experiencing the love of Christ through each other. Many people we know who aren't Christians commented on how well our church family loved us. And that's what made the Gospel and the love of God attractive to them."

**I was sick and you took care of Me.
(Matthew 25:36)**

How can I be Your hands and feet, Jesus?

If I Can Help Somebody...

In 1968, Rev. Martin Luther King Jr. gave a speech that touched on the natural human desire to receive praise as well as the way in which he would like to be remembered after his own death. He ended his talk with these beautiful and poetic words that we can all use for guidance:

"If I can help somebody as I pass along,

If I can cheer somebody with a word or song,

If I can show somebody he's traveling wrong,

Then my living will not be in vain.

If I can do my duty as a Christian ought,

If I can bring salvation to a world once wrought,

If I can spread the message as the Master taught,

Then my living will not be in vain."

I therefore, the prisoner in the Lord, beg you to lead a life worthy of the calling to which you have been called, with all humility and gentleness, with patience, bearing with one another in love, making every effort to maintain the unity of the Spirit in the bond of peace. (Ephesians 4:1-6)

Guide me in living a meaningful life, Heavenly Father.

Patricia Heaton's Vision, Part One

When Emmy Award-winning actress Patricia Heaton got time off from filming her hit sitcom "The Middle," she traveled to Zambia in Africa to build bicycles and make soy milk, among other things. The trip was in support of World Vision, a Christian charity that works with children, families, and communities around the world to combat poverty and injustice.

During a "Christopher Closeup" interview, Heaton explained that she went with her son, "who lives a pretty nice life in California, [so he could see] how a large number of people in the world live with no electricity, and who are just now getting clean water and wells."

They also witnessed many of World Vision's programs in action, including mothers' nutrition projects, the construction of medical clinics, and savings clubs which, says Heaton, allow women to "take out loans, start businesses, build onto their house, and buy goats and animals." It was a life-changing trip for Heaton, who returned home with a new spiritual perspective. More on that tomorrow.

Those who are generous are blessed. (Proverbs 22:9)

How can I help someone in need today, Jesus?

Patricia Heaton's Vision, Part Two

Actress Patricia Heaton's trip to Zambia on behalf of World Vision not only gave her a sense that she was improving the lives of those in need, but also a new perspective on the way she lives—and the way all Americans live.

During a "Christopher Closeup" interview, she said, "I came home more determined to simplify my life and clear out a lot of the clutter... I think it is a reminder of how much we've been given in this country. Just being born on this soil is a huge gift because no matter what level you were born at economically, you can have opportunities.

"I saw people in Zambia who were fairly gifted with talents and had dreams of wanting to do certain things that they were not able to do because of where they live. We can get so angry and frustrated and entitled here when Starbucks doesn't have soy milk. It ruins our day. So to see people who really struggle but have the joy of the Lord in them was extremely humbling and definitely has made me go back to basics with my faith."

Where your treasure is, there your heart will be also. (Matthew 6:21)

Help me to clear out the clutter in my life, Father.

'Your Child is Perfect'

When Courtney Baker's doctor diagnosed her unborn child with Down Syndrome, he encouraged her to terminate the pregnancy, saying her quality of life would suffer. Upset by his suggestion, she declined and gave birth to a daughter, Emersyn Faith. A year later, Baker wrote a letter to the aforementioned doctor, countering his negative outlook with her positive one:

"I'm sad the tiny beating hearts you see every day don't fill you with a perpetual awe...Emersyn has not only added to our quality of life, she's touched the hearts of thousands. She's given us a purpose and a joy that is impossible to express. She's given us bigger smiles, more laughter and sweeter kisses than we've ever known. She's opened our eyes to true beauty and pure love.

"So my prayer is that no other mommy will have to go through what I did. My prayer is that you, too, will now see true beauty and pure love with every sonogram. And my prayer is when you see that next baby with Down Syndrome lovingly tucked in her mother's womb, you will look at that mommy and see me—then tell her the truth: 'Your child is perfect.'"

It is to such as these that the kingdom of God belongs. (Luke 18:16)

Help us see the beauty in all children, Lord.

Do Our Failures Define Us?

Minnesota-based life and career coach Dennis Bird understands failure because he once created an unsuccessful business. On his website, he laid out the damaging effects of letting your failure define you. He wrote:

"Setting our self-worth and identity by our failures is a limiting experience. It limits our ability to see our life in the broader context of all that we do well and all that has gone well. Hidden in every failure is a clue to our next success. We need to let go...of the guilt and shame [and] discouragement. We can instead embrace a learning that will make us stronger and wiser."

He then suggests asking yourself these questions: "Why did I fail? What would I do differently if I could do it all over? What was within my control [and] outside my control? What is the key learning I can take from this so I don't repeat it? Who do I need to help me figure this out? Was it worth it, even though I failed? Nothing in life is wasted. From all experiences, both good and bad, there is something we can learn."

Though they fall seven times, they will rise again. (Proverbs 24:16)

Help me to learn from my failures, God of Second Chances.

The Meaning of Friendship

At age six, Ella Frech met a friendly five-year-old named Erika, and they were inseparable right away. A year later, Ella developed Juvenile Rheumatoid Arthritis, which left her on crutches and needing chemo to send her into remission. Erika remained a close friend. She simply spent time with Ella playing board games, coloring, or just enjoying her company.

Ella later developed other health problems that left her in a wheelchair. It was a difficult time for the Frech family that Ella's mom Rebecca wrote about on her Patheos blog. She said:

"When [Ella] was too sick to play, the other girls we knew lost interest and found other friends with whom to adventure and make believe. But not Erika. Through sickness and remission, able-bodied and paraplegic, this tiny girl somehow saw what even many adults could not—that beyond the sickness and the constant turmoil was a friend worth waiting for...

"I have learned from my daughter about the values of strength and perseverance, but Erika has taught me about what it means to love and to truly be a friend."

A friend loves at all times. (Proverbs 17:17)

Help me stick with my friends through thick and thin, Lord.

Love Will Heal

For several years, singer-songwriter PJ Anderson has attended the March for Life in Washington, D.C. Going back to his days as a youth minister in Chicago, he would gather with thousands of young people at the annual Youth Rally and Mass For Life, praising God from the stands and singing along with the artists on-stage.

A change happened in 2016, though. Instead of being a spectator, Anderson performed for 25,000 youth a song he co-wrote with his wife Rachel especially for the occasion: "Love Will Heal." During a "Christopher Closeup" interview, he said:

"Change is only going to happen through love. It's not going to happen by arguments or forcing our opinions...No law is going to change until people's hearts are changed. Only love can do that. There's a line in the song: 'We were all created out of the same love.' That love is God. We all deserve that same love. It's our duty to stand up for those who aren't being treated with love, who are disposable in a lot of people's minds."

Above all, maintain constant love for one another, for love covers a multitude of sins. (1 Peter 4:8)

I pray that our culture adopts a greater respect for life, Creator.

The Man Who Didn't Love God

Though he was raised Catholic, Jeffrey Bruno had abandoned his belief in God many years ago—and he certainly didn't love God. But he reached a point in his life when he wanted to finally prove that God didn't exist. He started attending Mass once a day and saying, "Hi. You know I don't love you, and it probably doesn't matter anyway, because you probably don't exist, but here I am. Amen."

Bruno went through 80 days of this same ritual. Then, something happened. Writing for the website Aleteia, he recalled, "All I can say is, God touched me...I felt a Presence that completely overwhelmed my senses and I experienced it: love, joy, peace—completeness."

Bruno concludes, "If you don't believe in God or you think He doesn't exist, seek Him out. Put your intellectual stuff to the side for a moment and genuinely seek Him. You don't have to tell your atheist friends you're doing it, but you owe it to yourself to begin the search, because if you find the Christ you will know joy. He will reshape you in ways you could never imagine."

May the God of hope fill you with all joy and peace in believing. (Romans 15:13)

Guide skeptics into Your divine presence, Savior.

The Polite Hostage Negotiator

For all of the 33 years he spent as a New York City cop, Jack Cambria had a secret weapon: he made up his mind to be a nice guy. He was polite. He smiled. He offered a simple "good morning" to people—all on the advice of his sergeant. "Goodness," he recalled thinking. "This works."

It sure did. When Cambria retired at 60 in 2015, after serving 14 years as head of the NYPD's Hostage Negotiation Team, he was able to look back on a career in which he had treated people everywhere with the same degree of respect.

"We learn from our past encounters and we always critique," he told Rocco Parascandola of New York's *Daily News*. "We keep the positives and move forward with those."

The Hostage Negotiation Team was formed in 1973—the first of its kind—and Police Commissioner Bill Bratton called Cambria a "walking history" of the unit. "He's trained hundreds of officers," Bratton said, "worked thousands of scenes, and saved untold lives."

Remind them...to show every courtesy to everyone. (Titus 3:1,3)

Remind me to use the secret weapon of kindness, Lord.

An Addict's Journey

Scott Weeman started drinking as part of a social routine. Ironically, that routine drove him to a life of isolation because it developed into drug and alcohol addiction. Now, he has started a website and ministry called CatholicInRecovery.com to help others going through similar struggles.

During an interview on "Christopher Closeup," Weeman recalled, "I found myself in this place where everything that was important to me—my relationships, my educational and professional interests, who I was—was all gone as a result of drugs and alcohol. I knew enough was enough."

Weeman reached out to those closest to him and tried to move forward, but he was stuck in thinking that God could never forgive him for what he had done with his life. It was a friend he made through a Young Adult Bible study who corrected his vision of the divine, telling him that he wouldn't be able to recover from his addiction without God's grace.

Other members of the group also welcomed Weeman with compassion and understanding, not judgment—and that made all the difference.

The Lord is merciful and gracious. (Psalm 103:8)

Help me to reflect Your mercy to others, Lord.

Building Confidence in Prayer

For many, prayer is a problem. People ask, "How am I to pray?" or "Why aren't my prayers answered?" or "How can I pray better?" It would take books to answer each question fully. But here are a few thoughts on prayer.

- **Prayer builds on human weakness.** God reminds us how much we need Him. A recovering alcoholic wrote, "Not until I turned my will and life over to God's care did things change for me."
- **Prayer promotes self-respect.** There is something wrong with your prayer if you concentrate on your faults. Self-confidence comes when you begin to believe that God really does love you for yourself just as you are.
- **Prayer rejoices in the presence of God.** A woman wrote, "In my fifty-five years...I have found delight in the Lord for I always have Him beside me."
- **Prayer is patient — *with God.*** You can't plant an acorn one day and expect to sit in the oak tree's shade the next.

> **I waited patiently for the Lord; He inclined to me and heard my cry. (Psalm 40:1)**

> *Christ, teach me to pray with fervency and sincerity.*

How to Drive Out Darkness

The newsletter *Apple Seeds* shared a story about combating evil that was written by Paul J. Wharton: "The students of a rabbi approached their teacher with a deep concern about the prevalence of evil in the world.

"Intent upon driving out the forces of darkness, they requested the rabbi to counsel them. He suggested that they take brooms and attempt to sweep the darkness out of the cellar.

"The bewildered disciples applied themselves to sweeping out darkness, but to no avail. The rabbi then advised his followers to take sticks and to beat vigorously at the darkness to drive out evil. When this likewise failed, he counseled them to go down to the cellar again and to protest against the darkness by shouting at it.

"When this, too, failed, the rabbi said, 'My children, let each of you meet the challenge of darkness by lighting a candle.'

"The disciples descended again to the cellar and kindled their lights. They looked, and behold! The darkness had been driven out."

Live as children of light. (Ephesians 5:8)

Guide me in dispelling darkness with light, Jesus.

An Astronaut's Legacy

Ronald E. McNair, one of seven astronauts killed when the Challenger space shuttle exploded in 1986, left quite a legacy in New York City. There's a playground in Manhattan named after him, as well as a park across from the Brooklyn Museum, and two schools, one in Brooklyn and the other in Queens.

More than that, there are the memories: a boyhood in South Carolina, marked by a fascination with space travel; a doctorate in physics from MIT; admission to NASA's astronaut program in 1978; and becoming the second black American to orbit the earth six years later.

Jason Silverstein wrote a tribute to McNair in New York's *Daily News*, on the 30th anniversary of the explosion, which also cost the lives of teacher Christa McAuliffe, Michael Smith, Francis Scobee, Ellison Onizuka, Gregory Jarvis and Judith Resnick.

Silverstein quoted Dr. Shirley Ann Jackson, with whom McNair became friendly at MIT. "We felt we had an opportunity and an obligation," she said, "to inspire others like us."

I look at Your heavens, the moon and the stars that You have established. (Psalm 8:3)

Creator, may I inspire others to reach for the stars.

From Stress to Slumber

When you're stressed out, the one thing you need to revive and rejuvenate yourself is a restful night's sleep. Of course, stress usually leads to anything but peaceful sleep. So what can you do? Julia Hogan, LPC, offers some tips in *Verily* magazine:

- **Set Aside Time to Plan/Worry During the Day.** The Sleep Health Foundation reports that scheduling time during the day to deal with problems can keep your mind more restful at night. Also, writing down your worries and promising to deal with them the next day can also be helpful.

- **Listen to Calming Music or White Noise.** "A Stanford University Study found that listening to relaxing music and sounds serves as a highly effective stress reducer. The Sleep Council offers a series of 'Nodcasts' with calming sounds such as birds, rain, and waves to help you fall asleep."

- **Try Deep Breathing.** "Research has shown that deep breathing directly counteracts the effects of stress on the body. Breathe in slowly through your nose, hold for a few seconds, and breathe out slowly through your mouth."

I will give you rest. (Matthew 11:28)

Ease my worries, Lord, and let me rest in Your peace.

Saved by a Jedi

Dorrie Nutall had already tucked her seven-year-old son, Luke, into bed. She also made sure to test his blood sugar level before he went to sleep. But for people with Type 1 diabetes, circumstances can change in the blink of an eye.

Fortunately for Nutall, Luke's faithful black Labrador, Jedi, sensed when the child's blood sugar fell to a dangerously low number. Jedi instantly grabbed the *bringsel*, a device used to signal the need to test blood sugar levels, and jumped on Dorrie's bed, laying there until she woke up to check on her son.

Luke was diagnosed with diabetes when he was two years old. Jedi began training to become a DAD (Diabetic Alert Dog) when he was only 11 weeks. The two youngsters practically grew up together, and wherever Luke goes, his Jedi service dog is always sure to follow.

"They love each other," Dorrie concludes in a Facebook post that has since gone viral. "[Jedi's] alerts often beat the meter and he saves Luke…But Jedi's job goes beyond alerting, he also saves Luke…from being scared; he is his constant companion."

Two are better than one…For if they fall, one will lift up the other. (Ecclesiastes 4:9,10)

God, bless our animal companions, true angels on Earth.

How to Write an Effective Letter

You can help shape public opinion if you take the trouble to write constructive letters to those in positions of influence. Here are a few tips:

- **Be objective.** Stick to the truth and back up your opinions with facts. Exaggerations, emotional outbursts, or extremes of any kind detract from your point and often cause a letter to be dropped unread into the waste basket.

- **Think things through.** Instead of dashing off a few meaningless lines, take a few moments to clarify and organize your thoughts. This practice will add punch to your words.

- **Write promptly; don't delay.** A brief note of praise or constructive criticism dispatched without delay makes a far greater impact than one sent when an issue is practically forgotten. Furthermore, postponement often means "never sent."

God wants you to show a personal responsibility towards the world in which you live. Letter writing can help you exert an influence for good.

By your words you will be justified, and by your words you will be condemned. (Matthew 12:37)

By my words, Lord, help me to bring Your love and truth to all.

Mathilda Beasley: Pioneering Nun

Mother Mathilda Beasley, a pioneering African-American nun from Savannah, Georgia, got some well-deserved recognition in 2016. The Savannah College of Art and Design added her portrait to the wall of one of its buildings.

Born into slavery in New Orleans in 1832, she married, was widowed, and eventually obtained her freedom. She became Georgia's first African-American nun and, according to the website GeorgiaWomen.org, "donated her husband's estate to the Sacred Heart Catholic Church of Savannah in order to establish an orphanage: the St. Francis Home for Colored Orphans, the first facility of its kind for African-American girls.

"Mother Mathilda founded the Third Order of St. Francis in 1889, Georgia's first group of black nuns...She operated the orphanage until her death at age 71 [in] 1903, when she was found in her private chapel with hands clasped and stretched towards a statue of the Blessed Virgin, and her shroud and burial garments folded neatly with her last will and testament on top."

You will hear the desire of the meek...to do justice for the orphan and the oppressed. (Psalm 10:17-18)

May my life's journey be rooted in faith, Redeemer.

The Barefoot Commuter

Like a lot of New Yorkers who ride the subway, 26-year-old Kay Brown doesn't interact much with fellow passengers, preferring to stay focused on her phone. But when a beggar entered her subway car, Brown couldn't help but notice the woman's bare feet. She told the *Daily News*, "Her toes were crossed over each other and freezing."

Brown asked the woman what her shoe size was, and she responded, "Seven." That was also Brown's shoe size, so she took off her ankle boots right then and there and handed them over. The woman started crying as she put on the boots, and she hugged Brown before moving on, expressing sincere gratitude.

Brown was left in mismatched socks—she didn't notice that when she put them on in the morning—but a stranger gave her a pair of gym socks to walk home in. She shared her story on Facebook because "I wanted to post something that made me feel really good, to let other people feel good and maybe pay it forward...[Now], my friends are...Facebook messaging me that they've been inspired to volunteer, and that makes me so glad."

I clothed you with...sandals of fine leather. (Ezekiel 16:10)

Instill me with a spirit of generosity, Jesus.

The Boy Who Loved Junk Mail

One day, as Utah mailman Ron Lynch was preparing for his usual round of deliveries, he received a rather unusual request. "A young man was standing there [in the post office] reading junk mail, and asked me if I had any extra," Lynch told *KSL News* reporters McKenzie Romero and Sandra Li.

This youngster was Matthew Flores, who would often scour junk mail bins for advertisements because he had no books to call his own, and the library was too far and expensive for him to reach by public transportation.

"At 12 years old, he didn't want electronics, he didn't want to sit in front of the TV playing games all day," Lynch noted with astonishment and admiration. "The kid just wanted to read."

Inspired by Matthew's genuine thirst for knowledge, Lynch immediately sent out a Facebook blast, asking if any of his friends had books to spare for Matthew. To Lynch's delight, his post went viral, and books began to pour in from all over the world. Matthew was most grateful for his newfound library, and generously promised to share his books with other children.

A gift opens doors. (Proverbs 18:15)

God, may we never underestimate the power of knowledge.

Parenting Teens with Honey, Not Vinegar

Parents often wonder why piling on punishments for their kids' bad behaviors so seldom brings about positive change. You can take away the car keys and the cell phone, but they still miss curfew and let school or family responsibilities slip.

According to psychologist and parenting expert Dr. Greg Popcak, the problem might just be brain wiring. A recent study from University College in London suggests that adolescents aren't yet capable of imagining negative outcomes, or of modifying their behavior to avoid punishment.

At his Patheos blog, Dr. Popcak says the research echoes a familiar proverb attributed to St. Francis de Sales: "You can catch more flies with honey than you can with vinegar."

Dr. Popcak advises parents to prompt teens with positive reminders (not nagging), like a text sent half an hour before curfew. Another important tool? "Catching your teens being good, acknowledging when they have followed the rules or fulfilled your expectations, especially when you know it was hard for them." Sweet results, for parents and for teens!

How sweet are Your words to my taste. (Psalm 119:103)

Father, help me catch all those I meet by doing good!

Getting To Carnegie Hall

Who really relishes the difficult discipline of daily practice, even knowing how important it is? Irving Fields for one. Not only does Fields, a pianist and composer, enjoy practicing, it's the high point of his day. "And I'm still getting better!" he told *AARP* magazine.

For instance, he was never able to play a certain Chopin passage. "But one year ago, I told myself that, despite the carpal tunnel syndrome in my left hand, I would learn to do it. And I did."

The musician's achievement through pain and struggle is all the more amazing and inspiring when you know that Fields is 100 years old. "When I perform, it's like giving a Carnegie Hall concert in a restaurant. People stand up and applaud. Waking up every day knowing I'm going to play keeps me young," says Fields who appreciates the music of Gershwin, Sinatra, Chopin and Kern, and has been playing since the age of eight.

Persevere, whether your goal is to get to Carnegie Hall or to get up each morning looking forward to a new day.

Happy are those who persevere. (Daniel 12:12)

Dear God, help me to discover and use my talents to the best of my ability.

The NYPD's Civil Rights Pioneer

Last year on Martin Luther King Day, *The New York Times* profiled a group of eight Americans. Most were well-known members of the civil rights movement, but one name stood out because of its unfamiliarity.

Samuel Battle (1893-1966) was the first black police officer in New York City. His white brothers had responded to his 1911 appointment by giving him the silent treatment—until one day he bravely ran into a crowd of rioters to rescue a white officer.

Nor was it easy for Battle to get the appointment in the first place. He had to retake the test, after an initial prejudice-related rejection, following a protest by fellow blacks. He went on to a career that included his appointment as the first black lieutenant, and retirement as a parole commissioner.

"I would rather have honor and character than prestige and wealth," Battle once said. "I can walk and ride the streets of this city, hold my head up, and look all men in the face."

There is no longer Jew or Greek, there is no longer slave or free...for all of you are one in Christ Jesus. (Galatians 3:28-29)

Creator, remove from me any trace of blindness to the dignity of all Your children.

When the Ice Breaks

When Shi'eym Lennon and Shawntel Wilson of Paterson, New Jersey, walked on the ice across the Passaic River, they had no idea that their lives were in imminent danger. Thanks to some Paterson firefighters, they were saved, but it was a close call.

Halfway across to Pennington Park, Lennon's foot broke through the ice, and Wilson tried to pull him out. "All of a sudden, the whole thing collapsed," he said, and they sank into the fast-moving river. As they both began to pray, they recalled the moments they'd had together since first becoming friends.

A story by Joe Malinconico in *The Record* of Hackensack tells what happened next. A man on shore saw them and unsuccessfully tried to save them on his own. He then called firemen, who rescued the boys with Battalion Chief Brian Rathbone and Deputy Chief Brian McDermott taking lead roles by crawling out to them on the ice. Shawntel Wilson, shivering and wet, had one thing to say to his rescuers. "I love you guys," he repeated, over and over. "I love you guys."

Save me, O God, for the waters have come up to my neck. (Psalm 69:1)

Savior, let me be a foothold to those who are sinking!

The Heart of Service

The alumni office of the University of Notre Dame asked a number of its graduates and present students to choose the "golden moments" of their experience at the Indiana campus.

Most of the replies were fairly routine—a favorite basketball game, graduation, hearing the band play the famed Victory March for the first time. But the answer of Kaitlyn Kennedy, Class of '16, stood out. Here it is, in her own words:

"After my first year at Notre Dame, I decided to spend my summer in Mobile, Alabama, as part of the Center for Social Concerns' Summer Service Learning Program, living and serving at a nursing home for impoverished elderly. It sounds cliché to say, but that one decision changed my life forever.

"My thesis and minor capstone are about caregiving for the elderly and terminally ill, inspired by this work. I learned that service is about more than just doing works; it is about relationships that give life."

Where you go, I will go;...your people shall be my people, and your God, my God. (Ruth 1:15)

Jesus, Son of Mary, help me to form strong, loving, serving relationships with others.

An Insidious Killer

Carbon monoxide gas is an insidious killer. This poison is formed whenever coal, wood, oil, or any other fuel is burned. But the exhaust from cars causes the most trouble. It is especially dangerous in cold weather when car windows are tightly closed.

Since carbon monoxide is odorless, colorless and tasteless, the exhaust fumes can easily seep into the car without being noticed until it is too late. Its effects are deadly. The first symptoms of headache and dizziness are quickly followed by an inability to move because of muscular weakness.

Poisons to the heart, mind, and soul are even more difficult to detect than the physical harm of carbon monoxide. Check and double check to make sure you are not taking foolish risks. Keep your life God-centered, distinguish between good and evil, be zealous in promoting truth and decency, and you will run little danger of being poisoned in spirit.

Keep awake and pray that you may not come into the time of trial; the spirit indeed is willing, but the flesh is weak. (Mark 14:38)

Keep me, Holy Spirit, ever aware to seek good and avoid evil.

A Radical Approach to TV

"Radical" may not be a word that you'd associate with a TV series on the Hallmark Channel, yet it perfectly describes "When Calls the Heart." The show's radical nature doesn't stem from edgy content, however, but rather from its embrace of stories that an entire family can watch together. That's why we recognized the show with our 2016 Christopher Spirit Award.

"When Calls the Heart" takes place in 1910, and tells the story of Elizabeth Thatcher (Erin Krakow), a young teacher who gets assigned to the frontier town Hope Valley, where residents are good-hearted people with a deep sense of community.

Krakow believes the show resonates with viewers because the characters are role models and because there are lessons to be learned from each episode. Executive producer Brian Bird adds, "The goal is to tell universal stories with themes like forgiveness, redemption, sacrifice, courage, and banding together to help one another. The characters on our show reflect those virtues and hopefully make a lasting impression on our viewers."

Support your faith with goodness. (2 Peter 1:5)

Inspire TV writers to create programming that reflects Your beauty, truth and goodness, Lord.

Changed by a Vision

Was it possible that a poor and sickly child would be granted visions and change lives? Well, in 1858, 14-year-old Bernadette Soubirous told the world that she saw the "Beautiful Lady" of Lourdes, France—Mary, the mother of Jesus—and received messages from her. But the youngster was met with anger and disbelief and mockery.

Skeptical church officials questioned her. Some people tried threats and bribery to get her to admit she'd imagined the visions. As word traveled that a spring of water was flowing from the spot where Bernadette had been instructed by the Lady to dig, crowds came.

Throngs sought healing at Lourdes. People also sought to see and touch Bernadette. She wanted no part of their adoration. Eventually, she became a nun and was given more privacy. Still she faced suspicion and skepticism. On her death bed, she was adamant: "I saw her. I saw her."

Hers was an inner strength and faithfulness that we can admire—and try to imitate.

I Myself will gather the remnant of My flock. (Jeremiah 23:3)

Jesus, may we always have the courage of our convictions.

A Chaplain Goes Above and Beyond

When a crane collapsed on Feb. 5 last year on a Lower Manhattan street, a man walking to work was killed while another was left seriously injured. However, there was one pinpoint of life and light in that otherwise dark day.

New York Fire Department Chaplain Ann Margaret Kansfield was in the area when she saw a bride in all her finery, walking to her wedding at nearby City Hall. In the chaos that followed the crane's collapse, Chaplain Kansfield knew there was no time to waste.

The bride, Nesh Pillay, 25, was on her way to meet her 27-year-old groom, Aaron Vanderhoff, at City Hall. Not only did Chaplain Kansfield throw her own coat over Pillay's shoulders and escort her to the building, but she performed the ceremony herself on City Hall's steps, realizing that in the pandemonium few guests were likely to attend the wedding.

As reported by the *Daily News*, Pillay said, "There was a lot of fear over what was happening, and she was just incredible, leading us through everything. She made it seamless."

When you pass through the waters, I will be with you. (Isaiah 43:2)

Savior, help me to see and be Your presence in the chaos.

The Unexpected Bridezilla

Monica Gabriel felt confident that she wouldn't turn into a tantrum-throwing Bridezilla as her wedding day approached. But then she convinced herself that she "needed" certain gifts from her bridal registry in order to create her idyllic, happy life. Also, her idea of the perfect honeymoon in Mexico was dashed due to news about the Zika virus, which can cause medical problems in women hoping to become pregnant.

Gabriel "sulked" and "scowled" that her marriage was being stolen from her. But her fiancé Joe finally called her on her self-absorption. Writing for *Verily* magazine, she concluded:

"I knew he was right. But it wasn't just the honeymoon stuff; I realized that it was the registry stuff, too. Too much focus on planning for the 'things' of married life had made me lose focus on the 'what' and 'who' of married life. In a month's time I would vow to love Joe for richer and poorer, with a standing mixer or without one, tropical honeymoon or not. And that was the real cause for joy and the only thing that would matter after we rode off into the sunset."

Love covers a multitude of sins. (1 Peter 4:8)

Keep engaged couples grounded in humble love, Creator.

'Work Won't Hug You When You're Old'

Bob Dotson traveled around the country for 40 years, reporting on uplifting "American Stories" for the "Today Show." His wife Linda maintained the homefront during the times he was on the road, and Dotson paid tribute to her on Facebook on the occasion of their 44th anniversary. He wrote:

"For marriage to succeed, you need to count on more than your fingers. Families thrive when their members invest in one another and spend time together. I'm away from home a lot, but...Linda makes sure I remember that work and life are not the same words. Should I come upon an interesting news story, I'd think nothing of staying up all night to cover it. Linda taught me—by example—to do the same for our only child, Amy.

"They planned 'girl-and-dad days' while I was traveling. Many a lonely night, when I [was] in a motel room, they'd call and tell me about the adventure that was waiting for me...When I got home, I didn't rush out and play golf with the guys. Instead, I'd give my family the same passion and love I brought to the written word. Work won't hug you when you're old."

Each of you...should love his wife as himself. (Ephesians 5:33)

Ground families in appreciation for each other, Father.

Kindness Matters

Each of us can change the world for the better by being kind. People who act or work as caregivers do that on a daily basis, so they could often use some kindness themselves. Here are some small but important random acts of kindness suggested by *AARP* magazine that you can perform for caregivers:

- **Pick up the person's mail or shovel their snow.**
- **Take the person's kids with yours to a movie.**
- **Bring your friendly pet over to visit an elderly couple.**
- **Send the person a "thinking of you" card.**
- **Put a ready-to-bake casserole in their freezer.**
- **Play cards with him or her.**
- **Take their old clothes or unwanted items to a thrift shop.**
- **Bring over a nice bottle of wine to share.**

Don't underestimate the value of so-called insignificant acts of kindness. Even your smile and friendly greeting can make a difference for someone having a bad day.

God...will not overlook your work and the love that you showed for His sake in serving the saints, as you still do. (Hebrews 6:10)

Bring caregivers the support they need, Father.

'The VFW Keeps Their Promises'

The Veterans of Foreign Wars has a program it calls VFW Unmet Needs—and Kyle Orian, for one, is glad that it does!

VFW Unmet Needs came swiftly to the aid of Orian, a 15-year veteran of both the Army and the Air Force who's been in Operation Enduring Freedom and Desert Storm. When he returned to civilian life, he suffered from nerve damage to both hands, chronic back pain, and a traumatic brain injury.

Orian applied for help through the program to deal with Post-Traumatic Stress Disorder, for which his psychiatrist recommended nearly a year's worth of treatment at a VA medical facility. Among other things, he received Line of Duty benefits to cover expenses while he was unable to work, and even got a grant to cover repairs on his car.

"The VFW keeps their promises, and we were blown away by how smooth and immediate the process was," Orian said for an article in the *Patriots' Circle Quarterly*, a VFW publication. "This experience has been a lifesaver."

Those who go out weeping...shall come home with shouts of joy. (Psalm 126:6)

Prince of Peace, bring comfort and care to all who are injured in war.

Homeboy Bakery

Phil Rosenthal is best-known for creating the popular TV comedy series "Everybody Loves Raymond," but in 2015 he started hosting his own food show on *PBS* called, "I'll Have What Phil's Having." Rosenthal traveled around the world to try tasty dishes in Italy, China, and more. In one episode, however, he explored food options in his hometown of Los Angeles, and managed to promote a worthwhile business/charity, too.

Rosenthal visited Homeboy Bakery, an enterprise started by Jesuit Father Greg Boyle in 1992 to help give young people a positive alternative to joining gangs. Father Boyle put these young people to work, teaching them both business and baking skills—and often having formerly rival gang members working side by side to form friendships instead.

Rosenthal praises Homeboy: "Father Greg Boyle's vision [is] to rehabilitate and help at-risk youth. They bake bread, run a cafe, make their lives better, and make the world better through their work, which just happens to be delicious."

Shun youthful passions and pursue righteousness, faith, love, and peace. (2 Timothy 2:22)

Direct young people to productive and positive work, Father.

'You Think God Likes Baseball, Herb?'

The Christopher Award-winning film "42" did an excellent job laying bare the racism that Jackie Robinson dealt with after Branch Rickey hired him to play for the Brooklyn Dodgers, thereby breaking the color barrier in Major League Baseball.

In one scene, Phillies manager Ben Chapman (Alan Tudyk) berates Robinson (Chadwick Boseman) with racial epithets during a game. For 21st-century viewers, this scene doesn't provide dry history; it immerses you in that particular time and helps you see the injustice of discrimination.

There's also an exchange between Rickey (Harrison Ford) and Herb Pennock, an opposing player who refuses to take the field with Robinson because he's black. Rickey asks him, "You think God likes baseball, Herb?" Pennock responds, "What's that supposed to mean?"

Rickey answers, "It means someday you're gonna meet God, and when He inquires as to why you didn't take the field against Robinson in Philadelphia, and you answer that it's because he was a Negro, it may not be a sufficient reply!"

God shows no partiality. (Romans 2:11)

Move our culture beyond old prejudices, Creator of All.

Putting a Positive Spin on Moving

Father Bill Byrne knows what it's like to deal with change. He's been moved himself, from a parish in the nation's capital to pastor of Our Lady of Mercy in Potomac, Maryland. Writing about it in his regular column in the *Catholic Standard* of Washington, D.C., he listed five reasons why change, especially moving, can be a force for good.

- **Sharing.** Citing the passage from Luke in which St. John the Baptist says, "Whoever has two tunics should share with the person who has none," he cites the value of a good cleaning out of the stuff we've accumulated—and of sharing with the poor.

- **Friendship.** Moving challenges us to keep up with old friends—and to make new ones.

- **No coincidences.** God has a plan, and moving forces us to trust in His care for all of us.

- **Strangers.** Learning your way around a new place "is an excellent meditation on what it means to be a stranger."

- **Resurrection.** "Moving helps us remember that life's little challenges are just preparing us for the greatest victory of all."

Trust in the Lord with all your heart...and He will make straight your paths. (Proverbs 3:5-6)

Make me open to trying new things, Lord.

The SpongeBob Maneuver

Brandon Williams, 13, a seventh-grader from Staten Island, New York, knows all about the Heimlich maneuver—and he recently put it to good use. Brandon rose to the occasion when he saw classmate Jessica Pellegrino choking on a piece of apple while she was having lunch in the cafeteria. He promptly sprang into action, using the Heimlich to dislodge the piece of apple, saving Jessica's life.

Brandon learned how to use the Heimlich not from a medical journal, but by watching his favorite cartoon character, SpongeBob Square-Pants, on *Nickelodeon TV*. "I watch it all day," he explained.

Brandon's not too verbal because he has autism, but his proud dad, Anthony Williams, reflected on the moment: "He did everything correctly, with the hand and fist and everything. We asked him where he learned it, and he always says the cartoon. Raising special-needs kids, you feel like they're very limited in what they can do. This just proves don't ever hold your kid back for anything. There's no limit to what these kids can do."

Whoever becomes humble like this child is the greatest in the kingdom of heaven. (Matthew 18:4)

Lord Jesus, let me never hesitate to use the humblest gift.

Helping to Feed the World

"We'll be dead if somebody doesn't help us."

A young mother named Fortunate Maangla voiced those words not long ago. And she meant it, literally. Her family and their neighbors subsist entirely on the fruit from the baobab tree, which is alternately sweet and sour. It quells hunger pangs for a while, but obviously is no substitute for a real balanced diet.

Dr. Carolyn Y. Woo, the president and CEO of Catholic Relief Services, told Fortunate's story in a letter, which listed some of the ways that CRS is helping to combat this crisis. For one thing, she writes, in Zimbabwe, "CRS and our partner Caritas Harare are providing farmers with drought-resistant seeds and quick-growing crops, as well as training to grow new crops and conserve precious water and soil."

That, she explains, will help farmers recover from loss and provide better nutrition to their families. That's part of the mission of CRS—all over the world.

If you offer your food to the hungry, and satisfy the needs of the afflicted, then your light shall rise in the darkness. (Isaiah 58:10)

God, help me to recognize and satisfy the hungers of those around me.

To Destroy or Build Up

Many years ago, a famous painting was ruined by an acid thrower in Munich, Germany. The masterpiece by the celebrated Flemish artist, Peter Paul Rubens, "Descent of the Damned into Hell," was an outstanding treasure of the State Art Gallery and was valued at $1,000,000.

It was never determined what motivated this destructive act. But those who are bitter rarely confine their evil to themselves. They often take a fiendish delight in forcing their misery on everybody else.

Vengeance, brutality, and destruction are being spread on a wide scale today. But there is still a great hope for a better future because it is against the nature of man to destroy. He was made by his Creator to build and he harms himself and others when he falls prey to his baser instincts.

Discover and nurture the innate goodness that still lingers even in the worst of men. If you do, you will not only accomplish great good, but will truly be a partner of the Redeemer Himself.

Good works are conspicuous; and even when they are not, they cannot remain hidden. (1 Timothy 5:25)

Help me, Holy Spirit, to find good in everyone.

A Tuskegee Trailblazer

When Calvin Spann was a senior at New Jersey's Rutherford High School, he left one month before graduation to enlist in the Army. He went on to become 1st Lt. Spann, a member of the groundbreaking Tuskegee Airmen, the black pilots group who fought in World War II. In 2015, at age 90, he was called home to the Lord in his adopted hometown of McKinney, Texas.

The Tuskegee Airmen paved the way for integration of all the U.S. Armed Forces, but it wasn't easy. Spann himself, as did other volunteers from the North, experienced segregation as never before—and he never forgot it.

He flew 26 missions during the war, but rarely talked about his combat record. He was a regular at the group's annual get-togethers, though, and, according to Todd South of *The Record* in Hackensack, was a favorite among his comrades.

"He was a very self-effacing person," said Roscoe C. Brown Jr., of Riverdale, New York, former commander of the 100th Fighter Squadron. "Very kind, smart and considerate."

Blessed are those who are persecuted for righteousness' sake. (Matthew 5:10)

May we judge others by character, not skin color, Lord.

Words to Age By

An anonymous writer took a humorous look at the aging process, making the following observations.

"Now that I'm older, here's what I've discovered:

- "I started with nothing, and I still have most of it.
- "I finally got my head together; now my body is falling apart.
- "Funny, I don't remember being absent-minded.
- "If all is not lost, where is it?
- "It is easier to get older than it is to get wiser.
- "Funny, I don't remember being absent-minded.
- "I wish the buck stopped here; I could sure use a few.
- "It's not hard to meet expenses; they're everywhere.
- "These days, I spend a lot of time thinking about the hereafter; I go somewhere to get something, then ask myself, 'What am I here after?'"

Even though our outer nature is wasting away, our inner nature is being renewed day by day. (2 Corinthians 4:16)

Creator, teach me to approach every season of life with grace and humor.

A Shocking Repair Bill

Bridget Stevens, a mother of two, returned home to a cold house one winter day in Moon Township, Pennsylvania, and knew there was something wrong with the furnace. With her husband Bobby deployed overseas with the National Guard, she called Paul Betlyn's heating and cooling company.

Betlyn came to the house to fix the furnace himself and discovered Stevens' family situation. Though she was worried about the repair cost, nothing could have prepared her for the shock when she read the bill. It said "deployment discount" next to the amount: one dollar. Stevens felt deeply appreciative.

Betlyn remained humble after Stevens spread the word about his good deed. He told *ABC News*, "My grandfather was a milkman during the Great Depression and many times he'd go to the door and the woman didn't have any money for milk. But the baby was crying in the background. So he'd put the milk on the table [anyway]. I heard about Bridget with her husband being deployed...I put the milk on the table."

It is well with those who deal generously and lend, who conduct their affairs with justice. (Psalm 112:5)

Inspire me to be generous in small and big ways, Lord.

Chaplains of Antarctica

Mass at the South Pole? Well, not exactly. But the "Mass at the end of the Earth" was the next best thing.

For nearly 60 years, the Diocese of Christchurch, New Zealand, had provided priests to celebrate Mass at the multi-denominational Chapel of the Snows. It's located at the U. S. base at McMurdo Station, on Ross Island in Antarctica. Now, due to budget cuts, there's a decrease in personnel—and a decrease in the number of people at the services in the chapel.

Father Gerry Creagh wasn't the first priest to serve there, but he spent 25 years in McMurdo, earning him the title "Chaplain of Antarctica."

Father Dan Doyle of Rangiora, New Zealand, will likely be the last priest to coordinate the chaplaincy program at McMurdo, spending summer months serving the scientists, members of the military and support staff there. He told *Our Sunday Visitor*, "[It's been] a great challenge in an amazing place."

Every high priest chosen from among mortals is put in charge of things pertaining to God on their behalf. (Hebrews 5:1)

Bless the missions of all Your holy priests, Father.

The Homeless Man's Gift

In February 2015, Jeff Daws was in Philadelphia with his wife, who was attending a medical conference. It was a "bitterly cold day," when he noticed a homeless man sitting on a grate trying to keep warm. Daws went to buy himself lunch and decided to purchase something to eat for the homeless man as well. He knelt down when he handed him the food and engaged him in conversation.

In a letter to The Christophers relating this story, Daws wrote, "He proceeded to ask me what my name was and I told him, 'Jeff.' He then said, 'Jeff, I'm going to pray for you.' I was immediately taken aback by his statement, then I asked what his name was and he told me it was Gary. I said, 'Gary, we're going to be praying for each other then.'"

When Daws told a priest about this encounter, the priest noted that homeless people have very few possessions, but this man gave two of them to Daws: his name and his faith (by telling him that he was going to pray for him). Daws came to realize how precious this meeting with a stranger really was.

**I was hungry and you gave Me food.
(Matthew 25:35)**

Open my eyes to Your presence in all people, Jesus.

The Gift of Caring

Marcy Cottrell Houle's father, who suffered from Alzheimer's, was literally forgotten after being transferred to a nursing home after hip surgery. He was placed in a room that was separated from the rest of the unit, so no one made a record of him being there—and he didn't receive any medication or water for close to a day. If it wasn't for Houle's quick action to get help after seeing him, he would likely have died.

Incidents like that prompted Houle to co-author the book "The Gift of Caring: Saving Our Parents from the Perils of Modern Healthcare," with Dr. Elizabeth Eckstrom. We were happy to honor it with a Christopher Award.

Houle said, "When people get sick or get dementia, they're often written off by the community or the whole system. Living through it as I did, it's sad and scary to see these changes. But the more you get to know them, you start to realize that they still are human beings. They still deserve a sense of dignity, and they still deserve our care."

Even to old age and gray hairs, O God, do not forsake me. (Psalm 71:18)

Give me the wisdom and patience to care for my elders, Lord.

Life in the Fasting Lane

We're used to fasting from certain foods during Lent, but what about bad habits? Peggy Rowe-Linn offered some advice on that topic for the West Palm Beach chapter of Magnificat: A Ministry to Catholic Women. Here is an excerpt:

- "Lord, please give me the courage to fast from anger, bitterness, and resentment. Please replace those words, feelings and actions with kindness, sweetness and lightness of spirit. Let joy be my companion."

- "Lord, please give me the grace to fast from self-indulgence. Please replace avarice and selfishness with the graces of selflessness and charity towards others."

- "Lord, please give me the grace to fast from constant and chronic distractions that separate me from Your desires for me. Please grace me with the ability to listen and be attentive to the needs of others and act upon those needs as You would have me act. Let nothing distract me from You."

Look, you fast only to quarrel and to fight and to strike with a wicked fist. Such fasting as you do today will not make your voice heard on high. (Isaiah 58:3)

May fasting lead to positive change in my life, Savior.

A Hostage Situation's Unexpected Turn

"I'm gonna die, and this is what I deserve." That was the first thought that went through Ashley Smith's mind when escaped murderer Brian Nichols took her hostage outside her Atlanta home in 2005. Smith was a meth addict who frequently promised herself that she would quit drugs so she could be a better mother to her young daughter. She would beg God to change her life—but when He did, she would do drugs again.

Now, Smith believed, God was finally done with her. But the opposite turned out to be true. Nichols saw the book "The Purpose Driven Life" lying on her table, and he asked her to read it out loud to him. During a "Christopher Closeup" interview about her memoir "Captive," Smith said, "He expressed to me he was a believer as well. He said that he was fighting a spiritual warfare. So I think he and I were both two people that were lost and trying to find their way back to God."

Smith convinced Nichols to surrender peacefully to the police. Since that night, she has been drug-free.

In Him we have redemption through His blood, the forgiveness of our trespasses. (Ephesians 1:7)

Guide me through life's dark valleys to Your light, Lord.

Godly Gumbo

During Leah Chase's childhood, her father taught her three rules for good living: "When you get up in the morning, you pray, you work, and you do for others." Since Chase is now 91, has been married for 68 years, and is known as New Orleans' "Queen of Creole Cuisine," those rules have served her well.

More than 60 years ago, Chase started working at her in-laws' bar and sandwich shop, called Dooky Chase (the family name). As reported by LoyolaPress.com, she wanted to establish a sit-down restaurant for African-Americans like herself who weren't allowed to eat in white establishments. Her changes—which included her special gumbo for Holy Thursday—made Dooky's more popular. It even became a haven for civil rights meetings with people like Rev. Martin Luther King Jr.

Chase's Catholic faith is evident in Dooky's as well. On the walls hang a birthday blessing from Pope Benedict and a picture of Pope Francis. And when she gets sore from working long hours, Chase says, "I ask Jesus to take that aching as a prayer. And my work becomes my prayer."

Whatever your task, put yourselves into it, as done for the Lord. (Colossians 3:23)

May I praise You through my work, Heavenly Father.

'Please God, Don't Let the Train Move'

Herman McGarrah didn't have time to think. He barely had time to act—but act he did, saving the life of an infant girl who had tumbled to the New York subway tracks below.

McGarrah, 54, of East Harlem, was standing on a subway platform in Times Square when the child fell while getting out of her train car. The girl started screaming. McGarrah jumped down after her.

"When I got down there it was dirty, I was scared, I was kind of shaking," he told New York's *Daily News*. "I said, 'Please God, don't let the train move.'"

It didn't—and McGarrah scooped up the child, one-year-old Tabrina Ferrell, returned her to her mother, and then climbed up himself.

McGarrah later told reporters that he's lived a hard life, battling homelessness, drug addiction and crime. He's had a job the last few years as a bus dispatcher, though, and now he's saved a little girl's life. "My life hasn't been in vain," he said.

**Be strong and of good courage, and act.
(1 Chronicles 28:20)**

When someone is in peril, Lord, grant me the courage and wisdom to help in whatever way I can.

The Good Samaritan

Brian Beutel of Westwood, New Jersey, was known as "the good Samaritan," and an apt title it was. In addition to his own charitable efforts, he was always teaching his five daughters to give back as well. Tragically, the veteran member of the Bergen County sheriff's staff died of a heart attack at age 47 while playing in a charity basketball game in March 2015.

An avid fan of the New York Knicks, Beutel was posthumously honored by the team during a game at Madison Square Garden in Manhattan. Former Knick player Vin Baker presented Beutel's wife Tamiko and their daughters with the Sweetwater Clifton Spirit Award, named after another former Knick player. The award came with a $2,000 donation to Beutel's favorite charity, "Tomorrow's Children," beneficiary of the game in which Beutel was playing the night he died.

The sellout crowd, there for a Knicks' game against the Milwaukee Bucks, applauded as the award was announced—and as Beutel's smiling family looked on proudly.

Teach us to count our days that we may gain a wise heart. (Psalm 90:12)

Creator, teach me to make each day of my life count.

Honest Family Returns Cash

Many years ago, two children, Daniel and Patrick Rein, found an envelope on the sidewalk near their home. They saw that it contained a lot of money and took it to their father to see what should be done with it.

The envelope held $2,200 in cash and some college forms, but there was no name on the forms. Mr. Rein knew that the money must belong to a student, probably someone who had worked and saved to pay tuition. He immediately phoned a nearby college.

The money turned out to be the life savings of 17-year-old José Rodriguez. He had dropped the envelope on his way to pay his tuition. Thanks to the honesty of the Rein family, he was able to attend college as he had planned.

Birds roost with their kind, so honesty comes home to those who practice it. (Sirach 27:9)

May honesty reign in both my heart and home, Savior.

The Beers List

Have you ever heard of The Beers List? No, it's got nothing to do with your favorite sudsy brew. Instead, it's a resource that can save the lives of seniors.

Marcy Cottrell Houle, the Christopher Award-winning author of "The Gift of Caring: Saving Our Parents from the Perils of Modern Healthcare," explained, "The fourth leading cause of death in seniors is called *polypharmacy*, which is too many drugs. What happens is that people go to one specialist and another and another, and then they get plied with a lot of drugs.

"What I saw with my mom at one point, she was confused and weak and tired. I thought, 'She's just getting old.' Finally, we were blessed that she could see a wonderful geriatrician, who looked at her medical list and [said], 'We're gonna get rid of this drug and this drug and this drug.'

"These drugs were on the Beers List, a list of all the drugs seniors should not be on, but are routinely prescribed. After those drugs were gone, my mom perked up and her cognitive abilities went up. It's a big deal! But people don't know what that list is."

Are any among you sick? (James 5:14)

Heal my physical and spiritual ailments, Messiah.

An Officer Doing His Job

You can't blame Officer Brian Strockbine of the Evesham, New Jersey Police Department if he's putting in for a bit of overtime recently. He's earned it—by saving the lives of three people in the space of only 10 days last year. If that's not a record, it'll do until one comes along.

The first rescue came on March 8, when an apparently dead woman was found on a lawn in town. Strockbine administered CPR, which was successful—and the woman's husband was arrested for beating her.

Then came March 12, when the officer was first on the scene of an auto wreck. He freed the driver, who was passing out, by breaking a window and dragging him out of the car. And on March 17, he saved another woman by once more using CPR.

Sophia Rosenbaum reported on the incidents in the *New York Post*, but Strockbine himself was quick to brush it all off. The 37-year-old put it simply: "All I was doing was my job."

A Samaritan while traveling came near him; and when he saw him, he was moved with pity. (Luke 10:33)

Redeemer, may I always consider it "just my job" to help those who are in need.

Where Your True Beautiful Self Lives

When "Nashville" actress Clare Bowen was four years old, she was diagnosed with end-stage nephroblastoma, a cancer the doctors said would kill her within two weeks. Her only hope was an experimental treatment, which also might kill her.

The Bowens opted for treatment, so Clare spent a lot of time in the hospital "surrounded by children just like me," she revealed on Facebook. "We were mostly bald, all tubed, taped, bandaged up and stitched back together....We were all together, so no one's appearance came into question."

Thankfully, Bowen recovered. As an adult, she remains sensitive to the fact that people—especially children enduring medical problems—may not fit our culture's standard of beauty.

Her message to them? "Every scar tells a story, every bald head, every dark circle, every prosthetic limb, and every reflection in a mirror that you might not recognize anymore. Look deeper than skin, hair, nails, and lips. You are who you are in your bones. That is where you have the potential to shine the brightest from. It is where your true beautiful self lives."

Let your adornment be the inner self with the lasting beauty of a gentle and quiet spirit. (1 Peter 3:4)

Help me to appreciate true beauty, Lord.

PB & J, Anyone?

Brooklyn artist Jessica Olah, age 30, recently displayed an unusual but heartwarming masterpiece. She assembled 2,340 peanut butter and jelly sandwiches, the approximate number her mother made for her growing up, to show her gratitude for one of the most frequently overlooked tasks of a parent—making your child's lunch.

With spectators watching, Olah made these PB&Js at her latest art installation over a couple of days, while her parents stood next to her, handing her the ingredients. Following the show, these edible pieces of art were donated to the Bowery Mission, a nonprofit that aids the homeless.

Daunting and time-consuming as this project was, Olah was pleased by its positive outcome. "What got me started [was] thinking about how my mom actually made me lunch every single day to bring to school," Olah told the *Huffington Post*. "I was blown away by her dedication in doing that...Part of this was recognizing, beyond my mom, what mothers in general do...and just bringing that attention."

Her children rise up and call her happy...Give her a share of the fruit of her hands. (Proverbs 31:28,31)

Father, thank You for the gift of our mothers.

Celebrating Purim

Special days marking religious events can be solemn occasions for prayer, fasting, and reflection—or times of frivolity and food. Sometimes, they can be both.

Purim celebrates the victory God gave the Jewish Queen Esther and her uncle Mordecai over the Persian leader Haman. Haman had plotted the extermination of Jews in Persia.

The book of Esther is read in the synagogue. And according to Stephanie Gold, writing in *Veggie Life* magazine, "every time Haman's name comes up all the children are encouraged...to make lots of noise." Noise makers called groggers are distributed especially for the occasion.

Food is important, too. Triangular pastries called "hamantaschen," literally Haman's pockets, are eaten. Gifts of ready-to-eat food, often sweets, are given to friends and family. Wine flows.

So yes, there is a time for seriousness and solemnity. But there is also a time for joy and partying.

Sing aloud to God our strength. (Psalm 81:1)

Creator, fill our lives with the joy that comes from Your holy presence.

Angry God or Merciful Jesus

The Tim Allen sitcom "Last Man Standing" recently took on a religious debate with intelligence and humor. The story involved the characters Kyle, who is religious, and Ryan, who is an atheist.

Ryan has been trying to get his nine-year-old son Boyd to admit he stole candy from a store, but the boy refuses to tell the truth. He mentions this to Kyle, who arrives to babysit. When Ryan returns home, Boyd finally admits to stealing. Ryan asks what made him own up to the deed. The boy says it's because Kyle told him about Jesus.

Ryan gets upset because he assumes that Kyle told Boyd that an angry God would punish him for lying. But Kyle explains, "I never said that. Boyd was scared that if he told you what he did, you wouldn't love him anymore. I said you were like my friend Jesus. Even if I do something bad, as long as I'm honest, He still loves me."

A humbled Ryan—and millions of primetime TV viewers—thereby learned a lesson about the mercy of God.

Great is Your mercy, O Lord. (Psalm 119:156)

May I use love, not fear, to spread Your word, Jesus.

Miracles From Heaven

In the inspired-by-a-true-story movie "Miracles From Heaven," Jennifer Garner portrays Christy Beam, the mother of 10-year-old Annabel, who suffers from a rare, incurable disease. When the girl is knocked unconscious in a freak accident, she experiences a sudden healing that leaves medical experts baffled. She also says that she visited heaven and saw Jesus.

Garner's own spiritual life was reawakened while working on the film, and it inspired her to start taking her children to church. When asked on Facebook what she now thinks of Annabel's claims, she said this:

"Every time people talk to [Annabel], they ask if she experienced a miracle. Having spent a ton of time with this little girl, she is the most honest, authentic person I have pretty much ever met. I would believe anything the child said. There really is an old soul in there, and a very calm, spiritual person. She's trying to share her story because people want to hear it. She is actually healed. It is a miracle. It's a beautiful thing to see."

Daughter, your faith has made you well; go in peace, and be healed of your disease. (Mark 5:34)

Bring healing and reveal Your presence to suffering children, Lord.

Escaping Iran, Part One

In 1984, Betty Mahmoody, an American-born Christian, traveled with her Iranian husband and their daughter Mahtob to his home country for what she thought would be a two-week vacation. But the Iranian Revolution had produced intense anti-American sentiments in him, so he informed her that they would never be leaving—and he used physical and emotional abuse to keep them there.

While Betty wasn't much of a church-going person before Iran, she and her daughter came to rely on God while being held against their will. During a "Christopher Closeup" interview about her memoir "My Name is Mahtob," Mahtob said "We couldn't practice [our faith] openly, but we prayed constantly. As a child, I was afraid of the bathroom in Iran because it was dark, smelly, and there were cockroaches. My mother would go into the bathroom with me, and that's where we would whisper our prayers, in secret."

Despite the trauma of what she faced, Mahtob says of that time, "God always puts the right person in my life at the right time." That part of the story tomorrow.

Pray to your Father who is in secret. (Matthew 6:6)

Grant hope to those in abusive situations, Prince of Peace.

Escaping Iran, Part Two

Mahtob Mahmoody trusts in God's goodness because of the people He has sent into her life. She and her mother Betty would never have escaped from Iran without them. She recalls one shopkeeper in particular who overheard Betty talking to the U.S. Embassy on the phone about getting out of the country. His response: "If you're in trouble, I want to help."

During an interview on "Christopher Closeup," Mahtob recalled, "He initiated this network of people who were working very hard to try to help us escape. Mom asked him how she could ever repay him. [He said] he didn't want any payment. All he wanted was to know there was a smile on my face."

When mother and daughter finally returned to the U.S., Mahtob embraced Christianity wholeheartedly. As an adult, it helped her forgive her father for what he had done, even though he never apologized. She said, "We don't earn God's forgiveness, so my forgiving him has nothing to do with him."

Unfortunately, the dangers Mahtob would face didn't end in her childhood. The conclusion of her story tomorrow.

Blessed are those who trust in the Lord. (Jeremiah 17:7)

Release me from the pain of resentments, Lord.

Escaping Iran, Part Three

In light of her experience in Iran and the anxiety she felt for years afterward, Mahtob Mahmoody had already endured more trials than the average person. Now, as an adult, she was facing imminent death because the auto-immune disease lupus was making her own blood largely incompatible with her body.

Doctors worked feverishly to find a solution, and finally figured out that she needed a transfusion of a special type of blood. Their local search in Michigan turned up nothing. After checking nationally, only two units of that blood type were available in the entire United States, so they were airlifted in.

That saved Mahtob's life and allowed her health to improve. She is grateful to the medical team that made it all possible, but she also sees a supernatural hand in her survival saying, "God's grace is such a part of my daily experience."

She hopes to continue sharing her story through speaking engagements and her memoir, "My Name is Mahtob." And no matter what else comes her way, she rests firm in the belief that "God uses challenges for blessings."

Rejoice in hope, be patient in suffering, persevere in prayer. (Romans 12:12)

Help me use my challenges to be a better person, Lord.

An Irish Blessing for St. Patrick's Day

Next to soda bread, there's no better way to celebrate St. Patrick's Day than with an Irish blessing. Here's one that was written many years ago by Father Andrew Greeley, and was recently featured in the inspirational newsletter *Apple Seeds:*

"May your faith be strong as a mountain wall, / And subtle as the early morning mists.

May you believe that God's power conquers all, / And His love through trouble and pain persists.

May your faith soar like a multi-colored bird, / And shine brighter than the blinding desert sun.

Because you know your prayers are ever heard / And Jesus waits when the final day is done.

And may God bless you, / The Father who rules the starry skies, / The Son who rose from the dead, / And the Spirit who comes in hope."

Happy are the people to whom such blessings fall; happy are the people whose God is the Lord. (Psalm 144:15)

Increase my faith in You, Father, Son and Holy Spirit.

Savvy First Grade Fundraisers

How do you think you'd stack up against the first-graders at Frances Xavier Warde, a Catholic elementary school in Chicago? Each student was given $1 at the beginning of Lent and told to think of how imaginatively they could put it to work.

When they were done, the money would be sent through Catholic Extension Society to a two-week summer camp for handicapped children in Louisiana. The results were nothing less than amazing!

One of the most creative ideas came from Laila Valenti, who teamed up with her fourth-grade sister, Lena, to put on a musical recital with Laila playing cello and Lena the violin. They raised an impressive $1,500! As reported by *Extension* magazine last year, the entire class earned more than $11,000, which was turned over to the camp and enjoyed by the children.

Said the operators of the camp, the Diocese of Lafayette in Louisiana: "It is our responsibility to love and care for those with disabilities...We focus on morals and values."

He has filled them with skill to do every kind of work. (Exodus 35:35)

Inspire young people to use their creativity to help others, Lord.

Garagiola's Holy Family Devotion

Baseball broadcaster extraordinaire Joe Garagiola passed away at age 90 in 2016. Over the years, he appeared on "Christopher Closeup" twice and made a wonderful impression on the crew because of his friendly nature and joyfulness.

Garagiola was also someone to whom his Catholic faith meant a great deal. Former Director of The Christophers Father John Catoir recalled interviewing him during the early 1990s. He wrote: "We were talking about faith and I asked him, 'What do you say to those who claim that Catholics make too much of Mary?' He shot back, 'Father, I'm lucky, I know that if you want to get to the man, you get to the mother.'

"We paused to laugh, but he drove right on: 'We don't say enough to praise Mary, her care and protection. The same for St. Joseph, the patron saint of families. I always pray to him to protect my family, to put his arms around us. He took care of the Holy Family, didn't he? What more can you ask?'"

May God grant eternal rest to Joe Garagiola—and may Mary and St. Joseph have welcomed him, too, with open arms.

Honor your father and your mother. (Exodus 20:12)

May I look to the Holy Family as role models for my family, Jesus.

It's Not Always Easy to Speak Up

The Stuttering Foundation might not be as widely known as more famous support groups. Nevertheless, it plays a significant role in the lives of those who rely on its assistance.

Many people, even professional TV broadcasters, have struggled and surmounted speech impediments throughout life. John Stossel is a TV reporter highlighted by the Foundation as someone who overcame stuttering with speech therapy, support, and ongoing practice.

According to *AM/New York*, The Stuttering Foundation now has "a stuttering ID card" useful for people who have trouble speaking in stressful situations. It's available for download from www.stutteringhelp.org.

Lori Melnitsky, a speech and language pathologist quoted in the story, said the card helps people who are afraid they won't be clearly understood.

And remember, Moses was believed to have a problem with stuttering. Yet God made him a prophet for the ages.

Moses said to the Lord, "O my Lord...I am slow of speech and slow of tongue." (Exodus 4:10)

Holy Spirit, when I struggle to say the right words, guide my speech so I can do Your will.

Dressed for Genuine Success

Meet a teenager who calls herself a recovering junkie. She says she was hooked on designer clothes!

Expensive clothes made her feel important, so she spent much of her time and money on them. She didn't realize that a clothing obsession could become an addiction until she learned that a friend resorted to shoplifting to get his many designer outfits.

This young woman decided to break her bad habit by switching to inexpensive clothing. Then, she would use the money she had saved to treat herself to Broadway shows and art museums.

Now she has real interests and doesn't need what she calls "make-believe self-importance." She says, "I no longer look the part, because I'm too busy living it."

This young woman recognized a destructive habit and took steps to free herself from it. Is there anything we depend on more than is good for us?

**For freedom Christ has set us free.
(Galatians 5:1)**

Divine Liberator, free us from our bad habits.

The Lion of Münster

Blessed Clemens August von Galen served as bishop of Münster, Germany, during the Nazis' rise to power in the 1930s. But he didn't shy away from speaking out about their atrocities.

He condemned the Nazis for making the Jewish people scapegoats for the nation's problems, and for arresting and killing Christians. Then, in 1941, he gave three historic sermons.

The first denounced the Gestapo for arresting people in the middle of the night and not giving them trials. The second criticized the Gestapo again, this time for seizing property that belonged to the Church. The third sermon was the strongest of all. He reproved the Nazis' euthanasia program, which murdered people who had physical and mental disabilities.

The Nazis argued that these lives were disposable because they were unproductive, but Bishop von Galen insisted that all human beings had the right to life. He became so popular with his people that Hitler's regime was afraid to arrest him—and he did survive the war. Today, he is remembered for his outspoken courage and is being considered for sainthood.

I fear no evil; for You are with me. (Psalm 23:4)

Help me speak up for the oppressed, Prince of Peace.

Feeling Grateful After an ER Visit

"I don't know when the doctor will be able to see you," is not a statement Juliann DosSantos wanted to hear considering how much pain she was in and how long she'd already been waiting in the ER. That was the receptionist's message, though, so she and her husband finally decided to try another hospital.

Writing on her blog for the newspaper *Catholic New York*, DosSantos said, "I was at a very low point—in horrible pain, tired from not sleeping, stressed and angry. Thankfully, the next hospital took us, literally, as soon as they looked at me as we walked in the door. They were kind and treated me right away. It turned out I had a kidney stone."

Despite the troubles she endured, DosSantos ended the night feeling grateful. Why? "Because I had my husband by my side and I had friends and family sending me messages asking if I was okay. I had kind doctors and nurses who knew what to do...I was being shown love and mercy and compassion by the people around me. They were acting as Jesus in my life."

May you be blessed by the Lord for showing me compassion! (1 Samuel 23:21)

Jesus, may I reflect Your love to someone today.

Awakening the Force—and Good Memories

When the movie "Star Wars: The Force Awakens" opened in theaters in 2015, it raked in millions of dollars in business. The Christophers' Director of Communications, Tony Rossi, believes the reason for the film's success goes beyond simple pop culture nostalgia.

He writes, "'Star Wars' is popular among 40-somethings like me because we saw the original when we were kids and it captured our imaginations. But we were likely so young at the time, we wouldn't have gone to the theater by ourselves. For myself, I remember my father taking me to Manhattan to see it. We had never gone to the city to see a movie, so this was something special. I suspect a lot of other people my age have similar memories.

"As such, part of the draw of 'Star Wars' is the memory of the family we saw it with. It's not just about feeling seven years old again, but feeling seven and re-experiencing just a touch of our lives back then with the family that raised us and loved us and made us feel secure."

I thank my God every time I remember you. (Philippians 1:3)

Bless the family members who made me feel loved, Jesus.

From Selma to Montgomery

A special issue of the *Edmundite Missions Newsletter* a couple of years ago marked the 50th anniversary of the civil rights marches from Selma to Montgomery, Alabama. As hard as it may be for the old-timers among us to believe, it was back in 1965 that the famous marches took place, forming a key part of the civil rights struggle.

"When I consider the courage and persistence of the men and women who fought that fight, I feel deeply humbled," said the director of missions for the Edmundite Fathers, Chad McEachern. The Edmundites have their headquarters in Selma, and founded their missions' bureau in 1937.

Among those honored at the organization's *Gaudium et Spes* (Joy and Hope) dinner in 2015 was Luci Baines Johnson, daughter of former President Lyndon Johnson, who shared a familial tidbit with the audience: "To be part of this heritage is a great gift in my life. My father signed the Civil Rights Act on my 17th birthday!"

Has not one God created us? (Malachi 2:10)

Lord, help us see past the superficial differences that separate us. Unite us as Your children.

Make Movies That Matter

"Pete, you've got to make movies that matter," producer Pete Shilaimon's mother told him when he got into the film business years ago. With "Risen"—the story of a Roman soldier who comes to believe in Jesus after the resurrection—he knew he had finally made his mother's wish come true.

The religious aspect of the story was especially important to Shilaimon's parents because they are Iraqi Chaldean Catholics who escaped that country during the Iran-Iraq war in 1980 because of persecution.

Shilaimon told *Catholic Digest's* Lori Hadacek Chaplin, "My father literally lost everything we had...He knew that if we didn't leave, my older brothers, ages 13 and 11, and I would probably have ended up dead. It also was becoming more and more difficult to practice our Catholic faith in Iraq."

Today, Shilaimon is grateful for the opportunity to make movies "about love, hope, and all of those wonderful things that make us human."

I will instruct you and teach you the way you should go. (Psalm 32:8)

Guide me towards meaningful work, Holy Spirit.

The Compassion of God

In 2016, clinical psychologist and president of Catholic Charities USA, Sister Donna Markham, OP, PhD, sent a Lenten message to supporters in which she shared the following story: "Lent provides us with precious reflective moments to ponder what the great commandment demands of us: to love God with everything in us and to love our neighbor as we try to love ourselves...

"Last winter, a co-worker at the hospital lost everything she owned in a house fire. Many of us extended help to her but what struck me most was the action of a janitor who worked on the unit. Having saved a long time for it, he had just purchased a beautiful leather jacket and proudly wore it to work on the same day our co-worker had lost everything.

"Without a word, he took off his new jacket, wrapped it around her, and told her to keep it. 'You need this more than I do,' he whispered. For me, that janitor was a living expression of the compassion of God."

The Lord has comforted His people, and will have compassion on His suffering ones. (Isaiah 49:13)

Make me a living expression of Your compassion, Jesus.

Belated Honors for Vets

New Jersey veterans of wars ranging from World War I to current operations in Afghanistan received special medals from their state last year, and were proud to do so. As Todd South observed in *The Record* of Hackensack, some "took shaky steps...while others strode forward quickly, their faces as fresh as when they left the military."

Thirty veterans took part in this ceremony, which was hosted by New Jersey's Department of Military and Veterans Affairs. The ritual goes back a long way: to 1858. It originated as a way of honoring those who served in what has become the state's National Guard. Since 1988, when it was revived, the ceremony has been held regularly, and more than 40,000 veterans have received medals.

Among those honored last year were Harry Parker, wounded in France during World War I (the award was presented posthumously and accepted by his sons), and George Bruno, 89, a Navy seaman first class during World War II. One honoree called the ceremony "humbling."

These are they who have come out of the great ordeal. (Revelation 7:14)

Lord of Hosts, protect all those who defend us in battle.

A Saint-in-Training

Never call yourself a bad person, but rather "a saint-in-training." That's the advice of former Director of The Christophers Father John Catoir, and it's a truth he learned from his years counseling people as part of his priestly ministry.

During a "Christopher Closeup" interview, Father Catoir noted that "doctors have lots of evidence to show that negative thinking will destroy your mental health." Many hours of counseling ordinary people about their problems, as well as several years leading a ministry for recovering addicts called Eva's Village, allowed him to see that evidence first-hand.

He said, "If you have a belief that you're not a good person, even though you're trying to be good, that undermines your mental health—and it has to be rooted out. If you can't say you're a saint, you can say, 'I'm a saint-in-training. I'm a good person, and I'm trying to get better.' But there's no way that you should say you're a bad person because God made you, and everything God made is good."

God saw everything that He had made, and indeed, it was very good. (Genesis 1:31)

Increase my sense of self-worth, Divine Creator.

Choose Your Words Wisely

"Our words have the power to heal or to destroy. Our words can enhance our reputations or destroy our reputations. Our words can build relationships or tear them down."

Pastor Dave Willis of Stevens Creek Church in Augusta, Georgia, shared those words on his Patheos blog not just as advice for what we say in conversation, but in regard to what we post on social media. He admits cringing at what some people write on Facebook and believes all people have a responsibility to use their words wisely.

Therefore, Pastor Willis suggests asking yourself four questions before you post any messages: "Would I want my children (or future children) to see this? Is it true, is it kind and is it necessary? Is this post/picture aimed at sharing my life or just bragging about my life? Could this post harm my relationships, my reputation or my career in some way?"

On the day of judgment you will have to give an account for every careless word you utter. (Matthew 12:36)

Remind me to use my words responsibly, Word Made Flesh.

What Makes a Good Teacher?

Junior high school students gave their views on what makes a good teacher. The qualities that they regard as important are not only ability and technical "know-how" in the classroom, but also interest in—and sympathy for—all students.

One ninth-grader summed it up by saying that the teacher "should have patience and understanding of all students, and not show favoritism."

Every human being yearns to be treated justly and kindly. This inborn desire is instilled by God Himself.

Most of us are quick to notice any deviation from this divine standard on the part of others, whether they be fellow workers, parents, teachers, or complete strangers. But we are often remiss in showing a similar consideration for these same people. A refreshing change for the better is bound to take place once we are as prompt to apply this criterion to our own relationships with others.

We know that You are a teacher who has come from God. (John 3:2)

Remind me, Holy Spirit, to develop in myself the qualities I expect in others.

God in the Box Seats

The Minnesota Twins' management has added a Sunday Mass to their baseball schedule. The liturgy was introduced April 17 of last year with a Mass before the game between the Twins and the visiting Los Angeles Angels.

Ballplayers, coaches and stadium workers are invited to attend the Masses, which are held each Sunday during the season when the Twins are in town. According to *The Catholic Spirit*, newspaper of the St. Paul-Minneapolis Archdiocese, two dozen other Major League teams have Masses before home games in a program organized by Catholic Athletes for Christ (CAC).

Ray McKenna, CAC president, hailed the addition of Minnesota to the roster. "So often because of the rigors of the schedule, Catholic athletes aren't able to get to Mass," he said. "Stadium workers, too, have to be at the ballpark early and aren't able to get to Mass at their home parish."

With this new schedule, the love of the game can be combined with the love of God.

Remember the Sabbath day, and keep it holy. (Exodus 20:8)

Creator, may all people celebrate the Sabbath in peace.

Turn Fear Into Trust and Peace

On his Grace Pending blog, Tom Zampino acknowledges the influence of St. Francis de Sales on his own spirituality. In an era when many believed that the only path to holiness was abandoning the ordinary things of life, Francis demonstrated that our daily work and interactions could move us closer to God.

Zampino then shared the following prayer by St. Francis to help readers trust in God more deeply: "Be at Peace. Do not look forward in fear to the changes of life; rather look to them with full hope as they arise. God, whose very own you are, will deliver you from out of them. He has kept you hitherto, and He will lead you safely through all things; and when you cannot stand it, God will bury you in His arms.

"Do not fear what may happen tomorrow; the same everlasting Father who cares for you today will take care of you then and everyday. He will either shield you from suffering, or will give you unfailing strength to bear it. Be at peace, and put aside all anxious thoughts and imagination."

The Lord lift up His countenance upon you, and give you peace. (Numbers 6:26)

Help me to see Your presence in my life today, Jesus.

Beauty Through the Ashes

"I've learned that when God promises beauty through the ashes, He means it." So says Taya Kyle, who learned that lesson the hard way. Taya is the widow of Iraq War veteran and "American Sniper" Chris Kyle, who was murdered in 2013, by a veteran he was trying to help.

Despite the sadness and bitterness that linger from her loss, Taya's belief in God's goodness remains strong as she focuses on being the best mom possible to her son and daughter, while also preserving Chris's legacy by helping other military families.

Taya experienced some of that beauty in the way her friends rallied around her in the murder's aftermath. During a "Christopher Closeup" interview about her memoir "American Wife," she said, "My one friend and her husband got a babysitter for their three kids so they could be at my house, washing dishes for people and staying until 11:30 at night. She and another friend did my kids' laundry, stuff that I wouldn't even have thought about in that moment. Those are things that are seared into my mind."

He has sent me...to comfort all who mourn. (Isaiah 61:1,2)

When someone is grieving, Lord, help me to be supportive.

Paving the Way to Heaven

"Get dirty for God. Go lay a brick!"

This is the slogan of a summer mission program—a program in which teens help with projects like building hospitals and orphanages in developing countries. But it's good advice for all of us, wherever we are, whatever we do.

If you think there's nothing you can do to help on some worthwhile project, you're wrong. There's always behind-the-scenes work. This "dirty work" may not be glamorous, but it's important. Like buildings, successful projects are constructed bit by bit, from many small components.

Do one thing today. One letter, one phone call, one act of kindness—there are many ways to lay a brick for God.

Do you not remember the five loaves for the five thousand, and how many baskets you gathered? (Matthew 16:9)

Christ, may I remember that every act of kindness, no matter how small, makes a difference.

Out of Darkest Depths—Light

It seems strange to us that deep-sea creatures can live in perpetual darkness. As light passes through the water, it is refracted and the colors of the spectrum are absorbed. First red disappears. At deeper levels, yellow, then green, and finally blue, leaving almost total darkness.

Most fish and other sea animals that live at depths below about a thousand feet make their own light. In some fish, light is produced by bacteria in certain parts of the body. Other fish have special cells that make light. To survive in the darkness, these deep-sea dwellers rely on the light produced within them.

Disasters can make our world seem as dark as the ocean depths. To get through life's dark times, we, too, must rely on the light from within us—the hope that comes from faith in God.

They woke Him up and said to Him, "Teacher, do You not care that we are perishing?" He woke up and rebuked the wind, and said to the sea, "Peace! Be still!" Then the wind ceased, and there was a dead calm. (Mark 4:38-39)

Jesus, grant us hope in You and faith in Your loving care.

A Literal Helping Hand

Talk about brotherly love! Gabriel Filippini, 16, had it in abundance when he gave his six-year-old brother, Lucas, a hand—literally.

Lucas was born without a hand, and Gabriel, using a classroom 3-D printer at his high school in Virginia, was able to create an artificial hand (with the help of his teacher) to replace it. Lucas received the hand for his birthday in June of 2016.

By manipulating his wrist, Lucas is now able to pick up a variety of objects. In time, he will be able to do more things, including moving glasses of liquid or even tying his shoelaces.

"I wanted to see what he could do with two hands," said Gabriel. Lucas' own reaction was a little more personal. "It makes me think," he said, "that my brother loves me a lot."

I take pleasure in three things, and they are beautiful in the sight of God and of mortals: agreement among brothers and sisters, friendship among neighbors, and a wife and a husband who live in harmony. (Sirach 25:1)

Guide all siblings to treat each other with love and dignity, Holy Spirit.

A Coach Who Has His Priorities Straight

Along with all the other coaches in the National Basketball Association, Brad Stevens, coach of the Boston Celtics, has important responsibilities. Missing a game is all but unheard of in his profession.

Yet Stevens keeps his priorities straight. When he heard last year that one of his former players was seriously ill and in need of some "hard prayers," he skipped a road game in Chicago and went straight to the player's side.

He got to the hospital just in time, too. Later that week, the ex-player—Andrew Smith, 25, a leader of Butler University's Final Four teams—died after a two-year struggle with cancer. His wife, Samantha, reported that Smith's body had rejected a kidney transplant and sent out a plea for prayers.

"Stevens has a demanding job with high expectations," Bob Raissman of the New York *Daily News* wrote in giving Stevens his "Dude of the Week" award. "Yet even with the pressure and responsibility, his perspective remains intact."

I urge that supplications, prayers, intercessions, and thanksgivings be made for everyone. (1 Timothy 2:1)

Jesus, Healer, may I always answer the call to pray for others.

The Word You Can't Unhear

A woman wrote in to *Catholic Digest* to say that she had been praying for her son to return to the faith, but he was still caught up in a wild lifestyle and even facing a prison sentence. This mother wondered if God was hearing her prayers.

Msgr. Stuart Swetland assured her He was, and also shared this story "of a young man whose mother tried desperately to teach him the faith. He seemingly did not listen and began a life of gangs, drugs, and crime. Arrested at last, the young man, still a teenager, faced life in prison due to a killing in which he was involved. But while in prison, he at last came to his senses and gave his life to Christ...

"After his release from juvenile detention (a judge had mercifully not charged him as an adult), this young man became a great missionary for the Church. When he was asked what caused him to convert, he stated: 'My mother's example and teaching.' He [explained] that he had resisted her efforts, but that in her teaching, he 'heard a Word I could never unhear.' When he was down and nearly out, this Word became alive to him."

The word of God is living and active. (Hebrews 4:12)

Turn the hearts of lost souls to You, Father.

Flight Cancellation Leads to Friendship

Andrew Shumway's mom says he's a "people person," despite being confined to a wheelchair due to cerebral palsy. So it wasn't a surprise when the 14-year-old from Tomah, Wisconsin, befriended 19-year-old Brittany Klocke of Carroll, Iowa, when they were stranded at Orlando International Airport.

Brittany has a brother with autism, so she was sensitive to Andrew's situation. When he asked her to attend a special needs dance in Tomah, she agreed—even though it was being held the same day as her prom at Kuemper Catholic High School.

When the day came, Brittany and her mom made the five-hour drive. As reported by *Good Morning America*, Andrew was both excited and moved to tears that his new friend went so far out of her way for him.

Brittany, however, deflected attention from herself. She said, "This is about Andrew and the opportunities for kids with special needs. I would much rather give attention to families, any person with a disability and how amazing they are...They have the biggest heart and can put a smile on people's faces. They are just full of life and happiness."

A friend loves at all times. (Proverbs 17:17)

Help me act kindly toward those with special needs, Lord.

The Priest On Board the Titanic

On April 10th, 1912, Father Thomas Byles, 42, boarded the ill-fated ocean liner, Titanic, in England for his brother William's wedding in New York City. This Catholic convert was especially looking forward to the voyage. Sadly, Father Thomas's enjoyment on this trip was short-lived.

At 11:40 p.m. on April 14, while Father Byles was saying his nightly prayers, the Titanic struck an iceberg. Despite his own fears, during the last few hours before the ship was fully submerged, the priest heard Confessions, granted absolutions, and led the terrified passengers in prayer. He also helped many third-class women and children onto lifeboats, staunchly refusing one for himself.

Ellen Mocklare, a young Irish woman on board, spoke with deep admiration of Father Byles' "self-control" and courage in the face of such tragedy. His heartfelt litanies, along with the musical strains of "Nearer My God, to Thee," were the last sounds Mocklare heard before a lifeboat carried her away.

Truly I tell you, today you will be with Me in paradise. (Luke 23:43)

God, may our faith serve as an anchor in times of tragedy.

The Plague that Saved Lives

"You can't go in there!" the doctors at Rome's Fatabenefratelli Hospital told the Nazi soldiers who wanted to search two locked wards. "Those patients have K Disease! It will kill you to get anywhere near them!"

In reality, K Disease was an invention. The "patients" in the locked wards were Jewish families, whom the doctors and hospital staff kept safe from the Germans until the war was over.

For this courageous and life-saving action, the hospital was recently honored by the Raoul Wallenberg Foundation with a plaque displayed in the hospital courtyard. "This place was a beacon of light in the darkness of the Holocaust," it reads. "It is our moral duty to remember these great heroes for new generations to recognize and appreciate them."

Writing at Aleteia, Jesús Colina quotes survivor Gabriele Sonnino. As a four-year-old, he thought his time in the ward was imprisonment. "Today we know it was salvation," he says.

Save me from my persecutors. Bring me out of prison, so that I may give thanks to Your name. (Psalm 142:6-7)

Saving Lord, may I be creative and courageous in protecting those who are in danger.

'Because We Are Refugees'

When the terrorist group ISIS started attacking cities in Iraq, four Catholic seminarians from Qaraqosh were forced to flee for their lives. Thankfully, they found safe haven in Lebanon, where they resumed their studies.

On March 19, 2016, these young men were ordained deacons (a necessary step before becoming a priest). But the location they chose for this important ceremony was unusual. They returned to Iraq—specifically, Erbil—so they could be ordained in a church located in a refugee camp.

Remi Marzina Momica, one of the seminarians, explained to *Catholic News Agency* that they chose the camp "because we are refugees...People want hope, and when they see that there are four young people who will become deacons and...will be priests, that will give them hope and the power to stay."

Not only were Catholic leaders invited to participate, but members of the Chaldean and Orthodox churches as well. Father George Jahola, who is working with the seminarians, said, "It will become a communion around the altar, around Christ."

In the world you face persecution. But take courage; I have conquered the world! (John 16:33)

Guide war refugees to lives of peace, Divine Savior.

Where We Find Our Refuge

After reading about the seminarians being ordained in a refugee camp, Deacon Greg Kandra was so moved that he couldn't help but find inspiration for the homily he preached for Holy Thursday Mass. He shared his words on his Aleteia blog:

"We are a pilgrim Church. We are all refugees. We seek sanctuary in a world where it is increasingly hard to find—where the dust of life is being caused by terror and hate. Yet in the midst of this, we refugees are also reminded that our one refuge...is our God.

"The God who gave us Himself in the first Eucharist and who gives us Himself again tonight. The God who gave us Himself as an example—not on a throne but on His knees. The God who on Good Friday opened His arms between heaven and earth and gave everything...so that everything He had to give might finally be ours. The God who suffers with us, walks with us, bleeds with us and hopes with us...Let us hold this in our hearts. We are refugees—and He is our refuge."

God is a refuge for us. (Psalm 62:8)

When my heart feels restless, Lord, remind me that I can only find peace in You.

Widow Finds Purpose in Suffering

At 26, widowed mother Jennifer Trapuzzano has experienced more than her fair share of suffering. In 2014, her husband Nate was murdered. The couple had been married only 10 months, and Nathan was killed less than a month before the birth of their daughter.

In the midst of her subsequent anguish, Jennifer found comfort in her faith as well as motivational speaking, which she did at her former parish of St. Mary's in Muncie, Indiana. "I still always miss [Nate]," Jennifer told *The Catholic Moment* newspaper. "There's a part of my heart that hurts and aches every day, but it gears me forward."

"There is tragedy and there is suffering in the world, but it doesn't mean that God doesn't love us," she preaches. "God's love is always good...Suffering does have a point...a purpose."

"If you can't love someone because they've wronged you," Trapuzzano concludes, "look at the cross. Jesus has been there and done that...You can feel powerless in the face of these trials, but the reality is in your trials, you can make a difference."

We also boast in our sufferings, knowing that suffering produces endurance. (Romans 5:3)

Christ, grant us comfort and strength during times of trial.

Evil Does Not Win

On Holy Saturday 2016, Leticia Adams reflected on her conversion to Catholicism six years prior. Writing on her Patheos blog, she said, "It has truly been a long, wonderful, grace-filled and extremely painful journey of love and mercy."

Adams also commented on the meaning of the day itself: "Today is a great reminder that humans don't always see the reality of things. For us on Holy Saturday, Jesus is dead, but the reality is that He is alive even as His body lay in the tomb...The reality is that He is busting open the gates of hell.

"The evil one will never stop trying to convince us that God is lying, but we have the Liturgical seasons to remind us of what God has done for us. Not only do they remind us of God's love, of the Holy Spirit's power and of Christ's victory, but they remind us that the devil is a liar and that all of his lies come from a place of defeat and fear. Remember that when that same fear starts creeping into your life. Evil does not win. The Cross of Christ has defeated it."

The last enemy to be destroyed is death.
(1 Corinthians 15:26)

Replace my fears with trust in You, Lord.

Christ the Lord is Risen Today

Easter Sunday is a special day for all Christians because we celebrate Christ's resurrection from the dead and the fact that He made our salvation possible. But that's a reality we should carry with us throughout the year.

For instance, Brian Bird, the Christopher Award-winning executive producer of the Hallmark Channel series "When Calls the Heart," shared the following memory on Facebook:

"When I was young, my maternal grandparents would visit us from time to time. One morning, I heard Grandpa Benson humming a hymn while he was shaving. He invited me to join him. I asked what he was humming and he replied an Easter song called 'Christ the Lord is Risen Today.'

"I was confused. It's not Easter, I said. This man, who was no theologian, no scholar, just a hard-working jack of all trades, had to smile. 'Son, for people who call themselves Christians, every day is Easter.'"

As all die in Adam, so all will be made alive in Christ. (1 Corinthians 15:22)

Thank You, Jesus, for the gifts of eternal life and love with You and those I care about the most.

An Autistic Child's Easter Message

An Easter play about Jesus's death and resurrection put on by 11-year-olds moved Laura Yeager to tears. Part of the reason had to do with the fact that her autistic son Tommy had a role to play, despite his struggles to communicate and be social.

His religious education teachers came up with a creative way for him to take part in the production. As Yeager wrote on the website Aleteia, "Tommy would hold cue cards for the audience, indicating to the congregation that we were supposed to participate, and when and what to say."

One side of Tommy's sign read, "Because by Your Holy Cross, You have redeemed the world." The other side said, "Jesus, teach me to follow You."

Tommy did his job perfectly, giving Yeager new insight into the Easter message. She wrote, "This child who has so much trouble carrying on a normal conversation with his peers, his elders, with everyone, was leading the congregation in the spiritual words of the play. God does make a way. He finds a way for those who need one."

He will make straight your paths. (Proverbs 3:6)

Help me to be inclusive to those with challenges, Lord.

A Doolittle Raider's Passing

America lost one of its final links to the famed Doolittle Raids over Japan in 1942 with the death last year of David Thatcher, 94, the next-to-last survivor among the mission's 80 airmen. Thatcher, a gunner on one of the 16 Mitchell B-25 medium bombers that took part in the raid, was also decorated for helping to save the lives of four severely wounded fellow crewmen.

The raids, mostly consigned to history books now, were led by Lt. Col. James H. Doolittle, pilot of the lead plane. They gave an enormous lift to American morale—shaken by the Japanese raid a few months earlier on Pearl Harbor—showing that the Japanese mainland was not immune from U.S. attacks.

Thatcher died in Missoula, Montana. His death leaves Richard Cole, 100, as the last surviving member of the raid, which was launched from the aircraft carrier Hornet. Thatcher's obituary appeared in *The New York Times,* and was written by Richard Goldstein.

For everything there is a season...a time for war, and a time for peace. (Ecclesiastes 3:1,8)

May times of peace outnumber times of war, Creator.

Her Baby's No Trouble

A young mother made an apt distinction between "work" and "trouble" recently when she took a part-time job to meet a financial emergency.

An employer nearby offered to let her work as many hours as she could spare. But she said her child needed most of her time and attention and she could not be away more than a couple of hours a day.

The employer, trying to be sympathetic, commented: "Your baby must be a lot of trouble." Quick as a flash, the young woman respectfully but firmly replied: "My baby is not a lot of trouble! He's a lot of work, that's sure, but that's not trouble."

Those motivated by a sense of love or dedication seldom feel sorry for themselves. Their tasks often involve heartaches and heartbreaks, but in one way or another they become a labor of love. When you realize the importance of fulfilling the particular mission God has assigned to you, your burdens will become easier. Purpose always makes a big difference.

Come to Me, all you that are...carrying heavy burdens, and I will give you rest. (Matthew 11:28)

Remind me, Lord, that I have a mission in life to fulfill.

The Origin of the 7th Inning Stretch

Ever wonder how some time-honored traditions got started? Next time you're at a baseball game here's one you can share with your neighbors during the seventh inning stretch.

Brother Jasper Brennan was the athletic director and baseball coach of Manhattan College in the 1880s. He was also the prefect of discipline. When students attended baseball games, they had to sit quietly or Brother Jasper would take them to task.

But he noticed that the student spectators were especially fidgety at one game. So he told them to stand and stretch. It became a regular event. And when the team played an exhibition game with the New York Giants, the popularity of the seventh inning stretch spread.

Some ideas catch on quickly. Others don't make it to first base. To give your ideas a chance, keep on slugging.

I stretch out my hands to You; my soul thirsts for You like a parched land. (Psalm 143:6)

Let every one of my hopes and dreams be a small reflection of my hope in You, Divine Friend.

Mirthful Math?

Okay, quick now—if you can remember your math teacher at all, the odds are it's not for the laughter that he or she brought to the classroom. Math teachers, as we remember them, were fairly serious sorts, influenced by the subject they taught.

Not so with Eliot Weiss of Brooklyn's Edward R. Murrow High School. Not only does he bring laughter to his lessons, but he was honored for it by the *Daily News* with one of its nominations for a Hometown Hero award.

"We're going to have a lot of fun, but they need to be on their toes and be prepared," said Weiss, 62. "They all know that I am very serious about teaching." Former student Olga Zhurakivska said, "My attitude towards mathematics was completely transformed by this man, who made math seem like magic—elegant, intricate, omnipresent."

Weiss weighed in on his long-term impact, too. "They may not remember the math," he said, "but they will remember to be nice to everyone. That's what I try to do."

May My teaching drop like the rain. (Deuteronomy 32:2)

Help teachers instill students with a love for learning, Lord.

School Bell, Wedding Bell

Some men ask permission from their girlfriend's parents before proposing marriage, but Tim Markwardt checked in with a different group. The young man from McLean, Virginia, had met Sarah Kratz, a fourth-grade teacher at St. John Academy, a year ago, and now he wanted to ask her to marry him.

One day, Kratz needed to take a quick break, so she sent her students to the gym teacher. When she returned to pick them up, each of her students was wearing a white T-shirt with a different letter spelling out, "Will you marry me, Miss Kratz?" *The Arlington Catholic Herald* reported, "The children giggled, and other teachers peeked out of their classrooms as Markwardt walked through the hallway and got down on bended knee."

Kratz said, "Yes." And regarding her now-fiancé's plan, she said, "I think he wanted to include them because even though I don't really like being the center of attention, when they're around I'm at my best. I don't have any kids yet so they are like a little family to me, and he wanted to ask their permission, too."

**Enjoy life with the wife whom you love.
(Ecclesiastes 9:9)**

Help me to be supportive of engaged couples, Jesus.

Joy in These Bones

It's not always easy for us to wrap our heads around the belief that God wants us to live lives grounded in faith and joy, especially when we're carrying heavy burdens. That's an idea that singer-songwriter Sarah Hart addresses in her song "Joy in these Bones," off her album "Til the Song is Sung."

During a "Christopher Closeup" interview, Hart explained, "We all have a lot of human brokenness. There is not one of us that is an unbroken being. And I think that we forget sometimes that the joy of Christ and the joy of the resurrection is something that once we believe—once we adhere our souls to that belief—it is something that cannot be taken away from us.

"We act like joy is a circumstantial thing. But really, joy is so much deeper than that. Happiness and contentment maybe are circumstantial things, but joy itself is not. Joy is born of the knowledge that God has sacrificed everything for us, even Himself for us, to prove His love for us, and we are that love. That is really the essence of Christian joy."

I have said these things to you so that My joy may be in you, and that your joy may be complete. (John 15:11)

Instill me with a supernatural sense of joy, Risen Jesus.

Homecoming with a Twist

Here's a story about two high school students who restarted a tradition at their school—and aided a worthy cause in the process. Amanda Witkowski of Saddle Brook, New Jersey, and her neighbor, Colleen Moretti of North Arlington, are seniors at St. Mary High School in nearby Rutherford.

These young women decided that they wanted to graduate with a revival of the school's traditional Homecoming Dance, with an important twist: proceeds would go to a fundraiser for breast cancer awareness.

They quickly won approval for the idea, and the dance came off without a hitch. The proceeds, about $375, were added to the $2,000 already raised by a walkathon, part of a fundraiser sponsored by the American Cancer Society.

The two girls, co-captains of the cheerleading squad at St. Mary's, were understandably proud of their efforts. As Moretti told *The Record,* a North Jersey newspaper, "[Cancer] affects hundreds of women every day. I think we need to put more awareness out there."

Let each of you look not to your own interests, but to the interests of others. (Philippians 2:4)

Show me how I can make a positive difference for someone today, Jesus.

Finding Work with a Purpose

When she moved to New York City after graduating college with a degree in communications, Courtney Nelson took a job as a bartender, but knew that she would eventually like a career that gave her a sense of purpose—maybe working for a non-profit, for instance.

Thankfully, she didn't keep that dream to herself, but shared it with a patron at the bar, who then connected her with Patrick Donohue, founder of the city's first and only school for children with traumatic brain injuries: the International Academy of Hope (iHope).

It was a perfect fit for Nelson, who started off working in operations and, now, marketing. She relishes the opportunity to work with children who might otherwise not get the education and care they deserve.

She says, "iHope is a pioneering institution that is serving as a model for potential schools around the country and the world. I see the difference being made in these children's lives every day, and it feels great!"

Prosper for us the work of our hands. (Psalm 90:17)

Regardless of my job, Father, allow me to make a positive difference in the lives of those with whom I interact.

Quality is Made of Details

What is the difference between a superb violin produced by a master like Antonio Stradivari and a mediocre one by less gifted artisans? Details! There are virtually no items in the making of a violin that do not affect its sound. Different woods are used for the back and belly, supporting ribs, linings, blocks, and other parts.

The fiber and density of each type of wood affects the pitch and tone. Because the thickness of the wood has a marked effect on the tone, it is crucial to cut and shape according to the quality and curvature of the wood. Even the quality of the varnish is important to the production of a full, rich sound. Stradivari had his own varnish recipe, which has never been duplicated.

In life as in violin making, details make the difference and enhance the quality of our lives. A smile and "hello" can make a stranger feel welcome. A word of praise can give new incentive to someone who's discouraged.

If I speak in the tongues of mortals and of angels but have not love, I am a noisy gong or a clanging cymbal. (1 Corinthians 13:1)

Reveal to me, Lord, how the "small things" of daily life can be expressions of charity.

Once in a Blue Moon

If you ever wondered just how often "once in a blue moon" is, here's the answer: it happens about every thirty-two months.

A blue moon is the term for the second full moon in a given month. Since a full moon occurs every twenty-nine and a half days, a blue moon is possible in every month except February.

And, yes, when the weather conditions are just right, the moon really can look bluish. Check an almanac or the weather page of your local newspaper to find out when the next one occurs. Then look up at the night sky.

When you do look to the heavens there's a universe of wonder and beauty God has given us to appreciate. Take a moment today to notice, to enjoy, and to say, "Thanks."

It is the moon that marks the changing seasons...From the moon comes the sign for festal days, a light that wanes when it completes its course. The new moon...renews itself; how marvelous is it in this change, a beacon to the hosts on high, shining in the vault of the heavens! (Sirach 43:6,7-8)

How beautiful the moon in its phases, Creator, who set such beauty in the vastness of space.

Homeless Woman Stops Robbery

It was about three in the morning in the town of Oxford, England, when a robber broke into Lush, a highbrow cosmetic store. Little did he know this shop had two unexpected guardians sleeping right outside — 29-year-old homeless woman Lottie Pauling-Chamberlain and her faithful dog Marley.

When Pauling-Chamberlain saw this man emerge from the store with a laptop and over 1,000 pounds worth of stolen goods, she decided to confront him, saying she knew he didn't work for Lush. The robber immediately left the merchandise and fled.

Lottie returned the materials to the store's manager, James Atherton, the following morning. In gratitude, Lush set up a fundraising website for their unexpected heroine. "Lottie is a beautiful lady," trainee manger Rachel Ross told *The Telegraph*. "We were greatly moved by her selfless actions, and we want to thank her from the bottom of our hearts."

Pauling-Chamberlain plans to use most of the money raised to assist the homeless.

If you...satisfy the needs of the afflicted, then your light shall rise in the darkness. (Isaiah 58:10)

Father, may we always remember to pay it forward.

A Labor of Love

Fran Rajotte prayed for a job in which she would have an impact on humanity. She got it and then some, with a medical clinic in Haiti that she helped transform into a thriving facility that serves an entire community. Now about to retire, she called the undertaking "a labor of love."

Andy Telli interviewed Rajotte for the *Tennessee Register*, reporting on her excitement with the clinic. "We had nothing," she said, when she started in 2006. "We just had a piece of land. Now we have a thriving medical clinic that offers a variety of health care services and a laboratory and a pharmacy."

When a group of midwives completed a six-week course for their certification and were honored at a graduation ceremony, Rajotte was able to be there from Nashville. "The community was so excited," she said. And of her original prayer, Rajotte had this to say: "When you pray for something, you have to be careful to accept what God gives you."

I am confident that the one who began a good work among you will bring it to completion. (Philippians 1:6)

Spirit of love, grant me the grace to follow through on each new beginning.

Marine to the Rescue

As usual, the Marines had landed and the situation was well in hand—artificial limbs and all.

Former Marine Matias Ferreira, who lost both legs from the knees down while fighting in Afghanistan in 2011, was driving home from his wedding rehearsal in New York City, his brother and future father-in-law in tow. Suddenly, he heard what sounded like a serious auto crash behind him.

The *Daily News* reported that the driver of the other vehicle was screaming for her baby after her car plowed into a median pole. "With the Marines, you are taught to be prepared and act," said Ferreira. "Thankfully we were able to make a difference."

While his brother and fiancée's father got the mother and her husband out of the smoking car, Ferreira ran to the car on prosthetic limbs, tore off a headrest, squeezed into the back and freed the baby from her car seat. The group stayed with the family until paramedics arrived.

"The prostheses were the last things on my mind," Ferreira said later. "It doesn't have to be a Marine. It just has to be someone with a good heart."

I am your God; I will strengthen you. (Isaiah 41:10)

Father, strengthen and guide me in times of trouble.

Communion Among Generations

An eight-year-old girl may not seem to have much in common with an 87-year-old woman with Alzheimer's, but the connection between Malena Jerge and her grandmother Catherine suggests differently.

As reported by the *Milwaukee Journal Sentinel,* Malena required casts and braces for five years to correct her infantile scoliosis. The experience taught her empathy for those enduring health problems.

Malena has been visiting her grandmother's nursing home, St. Anne's Salvatorian Campus, for many years, but Catherine has had Alzheimer's the entire time. That doesn't stop Malena from loving her, though. In fact, the girl decided that she wanted to celebrate her first Communion at St. Anne's instead of with her own classmates.

Her parish agreed, so Malena enjoyed her special day with Catherine and the other nursing home residents, who she calls her friends. Father Al Wagner, who celebrated Mass, "expressed thanks for life's many blessings 'from age to age to age.'"

Grandchildren are the crown of the aged. (Proverbs 17:6)

Help me to love frail and lonely seniors, Jesus.

Conventional Wisdom Wasn't So Wise

There was a time when it was conventional wisdom that people with intellectual disabilities couldn't participate in sports. Thanks to Canadian Dr. Frank Hayden and his research team in the 1960s, as well as others, that so-called "wisdom" was proven to be anything but. Writing in *Crux,* Inés San Martin points out, "The impediment wasn't lack of ability but lack of opportunity."

During Special Olympics European Football Week in May 2016, opportunities for young people with special needs were plentiful. The event took place in Rome at the Pio XI Sports Center and was supported by the Knights of Columbus. Teams from Italy, Poland, France, Lithuania, and Hungary took part, providing a model for integrating those with intellectual disabilities into the larger community.

Logan Ludwig, deputy supreme knight for the Knights of Columbus, explained that they partner with Special Olympics because they share similar values: "Fraternity, unity, and support to the athletes as a recognition to the human dignity of all."

Those who wait for the Lord shall renew their strength...they shall run and not be weary. (Isaiah 40:31)

Help me to recognize the human dignity of all, Creator.

It Looks Like a Steady Job

When Father Ed Fronske first arrived at the St. Francis Apache Mission in eastern Arizona in 1983, he recalled that people asked him how long he intended to stay. "Until you ask me to leave," he would tell them. Now, laughing, he says they haven't asked him yet—"but they might be getting close."

Actually, Justin Bell's story in *Our Sunday Visitor* makes it clear they're not "getting close" at all. "I consider him a part of us," says Jerry Gloshay Jr., an executive of the Apache tribe. Known as Father Eddie, the priest lives at the mission, but celebrates Mass at two other churches in the vast reservation.

A Franciscan originally from Philadelphia, Father Eddie's Masses are likely to include elements of tribal customs—drums, incense, feathers and smoke. But despite surface differences, he knows all God's children are members of the universal church.

As Father Eddie put it in a homily, "We're the Body of Christ; we receive His body and blood, and we go out to take His message and His power to the people."

We, who are many, are one body in Christ. (Romans 12:5)

Help me to see beyond superficial differences, Jesus.

May the Force Be With You

"May the Force be with you" is a phrase made popular by the "Star Wars" movies. And in the context of the stories, it refers to an esoteric religion that believes that everything in the universe is held together by an invisible force. What you may not know is that the phrase had its origins in Christianity.

In 2014, producer Gary Kurtz told "How Star Wars Conquered the Universe" author Chris Taylor: "In the real world, religion is identified by handles. You're either a Christian or a Muslim or a Jew or a Buddhist or Hindu. As soon as you say one of those words, you know what's behind that, even if you haven't studied any of those religions.

"We did have long discussions about various religious philosophies, and how people related to them, and how we could simplify it. 'May the Force be with you' came out of medieval Christianity, where 'May God go with you' was a symbol that you would be safe. We wanted something as simple as that, an everyday expression that linked to the power of the Force that wasn't overbearing."

Do not fear, for I am with you. (Isaiah 41:10)

I trust that You are at my side always, Father.

How Am I Going to Do My Job?

He remembers thinking about his job the day he was shot. That was on the Fourth of July back in 2013, and the first thing he thought about when he took a bullet in the knee while on patrol that day was, "How am I going to do my job now as an officer with the NYPD?"

Jamil Sarwar needn't have worried. Oh, it took hard work, and a full year of grueling physical therapy, but he made it all the way back, to full-time active duty. Not only that, but he was promoted to detective in February of 2016. And Graham Rayman of the New York *Daily News* was there to see it happen.

"I thought, 'I'm never going to be able to work as a cop again,'" Sarwar told Rayman. "But I tried my best and the NYPD helped me a lot. They took care of me."

Sarwar moved to the U.S. from his native Bangladesh in 2006 and became a citizen six years later. His wife, Lamiya, and his six-week-old daughter were on hand as he received a well-deserved standing ovation from his fellow officers.

Heal me, O Lord, and I shall be healed; save me, and I shall be saved. (Jeremiah 17:14)

Father, grant me patience and hope in times of illness and disability.

Hard Work Breeds College Success

How's this for beating the odds? Camill Fernandez, who was a senior at New York's KIPP College Prep High School last year, was accepted by 22—count 'em, 22—colleges, and she wasn't even breathing hard!

The *New York Post* reports that she credits a tough schedule at a charter school with helping her to overcome an addiction- and poverty-marked neighborhood in the Bronx. There's also the pressure of being the first in her family to attend college.

Among the schools offering her enrollment were Georgetown, Cornell, Barnard, Wellesley, St. John's, Boston College, Fordham and City College of New York. She chose Penn, where she's studying economics and international affairs.

The daughter of parents who immigrated here from the Dominican Republic, Fernandez was praised by her guidance counselor, Elena Zalaya. "Camill had a lot of challenges at home," she said. "This is a tough neighborhood, but she persevered. I don't have enough words for her. She is just a stellar, hardworking student."

**I worked harder than any of them.
(1 Corinthians 15:10)**

Inspire young people to work hard for their goals, Father.

One Creative Manager

For a supervisor or employer, group leader or coach, bringing out the best in others is important to the success of the individual and the team. It requires understanding people. As Joe McCarthy, manager of the New York Yankees during the 1930s and 40s demonstrated, it also calls for creativity.

One day, he approached his shortstop Frank Crosetti, saying, "I'm not satisfied with the way Lou Gehrig is playing first base. He is too lackadaisical. I want you to help me. From now on, charge every ball. When you get it, fire it as quickly and as hard as you can to first base....Throw it fast and make it tough for him."

Later, a coach commented to McCarthy, "I guess you were trying to wake up Gehrig." The manager responded, "There wasn't a thing wrong with Gehrig. Crosetti was the one who was sleeping. I wanted to wake up Crosetti."

Keep awake — for you do not know when the master of the house will come, in the evening, or at midnight, or at cockcrow, or at dawn, or else he may find you asleep when he comes suddenly. (Mark 13:35-36)

Help me be alert to my own apathy, Merciful Savior.

Wisdom from New Moms, Part One

"Nothing can truly prepare you for the joys and hardships of becoming a mother for the first time," writes professional counselor Julia Hogan at Verily.com. So in advance of Mother's Day, the popular website featured insights from a crossroads of women—"teachers, lawyers, social workers, and stay-at-home moms"—about lessons they've learned from motherhood.

- **Being a Mom Trains You to Schedule Like a Boss:** "Pre-baby, you can grab your purse, swipe on some lipstick, and waltz out the door. Now, running a quick errand is equal to an epic journey. Embrace it as a fact of life...Bonus: Although everything takes longer, time will also pass by faster than ever!"

- **You Don't Have to Enjoy Every Moment:** "Katie A., a lawyer and mom to one-year-old Nolan, [says], 'It's so easy to get caught up in wishing for the next stage—whether it's wanting him to sleep through the night, sit up all by himself, or learn to walk—that you forget to enjoy the stage he's in....I won't say I enjoy *every* moment...But every now and then, slow down, breathe in, and enjoy where you are with your precious baby.'"

More tomorrow...

**She opens her mouth with wisdom.
(Proverbs 31:26)**

Guide new mothers as they embrace life, Creator.

Wisdom from New Moms, Part Two

Today, more insights from new moms via counselor Julia Hogan and *Verily* magazine:

- **Flexibility is Key to Your Sanity:** "'One thing that took some time to learn with my first baby was that it's much easier to adapt your life around a baby than try to force a baby to adapt to you,' Kathleen says. 'Accepting the ways of my baby enables me to appreciate her uniqueness more. And that makes me a better parent, which matters far more than being on time or having the house perfectly clean.'"

- **Moms Are Each Other's Greatest Supporters:** "New moms discover that it can be pretty lonely when it's just you and a nonverbal newborn or a toddler in the terrible twos. Making sure you have a community of moms for support is crucial."

- **Having a Sense of Humor is a Saving Grace:** "Victoria, a teacher, [says]...'You can stress out about [the baby] crying or be grossed out by poop or phlegm and spit. Or you can try to view that particular situation as ridiculous and funny.'"

Her children rise up and call her happy. (Proverbs 31:28)

Bless new mothers with a loving and supportive network of family and friends, Father.

Rusty's Close Call

Rusty Staub, an old-time New York Met known for his slugging, generous heart and orange-rust colored hair, was honored with the Terence Cardinal Cooke Humanitarian Award at the New York CYO dinner last year—but he has more than the award for which to be thankful.

Staub was on a flight a few months earlier and suffered a heart attack. He is lucky to be alive, as he said in his acceptance remarks. "When I go to church each Sunday," he said, "I say, 'Thanks for another week.' I'm not kidding you." He added, "I'm going to continue the work I've been doing."

What Staub has been doing—as reported by Dan Pietrafesa in *Catholic New York*—is impressive indeed. He started the Rusty Staub Foundation in 1985. Its mission, as stated on its website, "has been to give children the opportunity to live full, happy and productive lives and to give aid to the hungry."

Since then, the foundation has raised more than $17 million and has served over one million meals each year.

Enter His gates with thanksgiving...Give thanks to Him, bless His name. (Psalm 100:4)

Guide me in using this gift of life wisely, Creator.

How to Live to Be 107

A woman who celebrated her 107th birthday in Jersey City credited her longevity to her faith in God and hard work. Mrs. Paula Rubin, a widow since her husband's death at the age of 95, was born in Poland. Ever since childhood, she has kept herself occupied with some useful work.

Concerning trust in the Lord, she said: "I have a deep and abiding faith in God and I guess He has had faith in me, because He has let me live so long."

Those whose lives are God-centered are usually motivated by a sense of responsibility to spend their years meaningfully instead of merely existing. As a result, they remain young in heart and also in body. They experience a joy in living that may elude those who only live for themselves.

Work hard during your comparatively few years in this life. Make the world better for your being in it. Put in as much as you can, and you will be building for eternity.

Each will receive wages according to the labor of each. (1 Corinthians 3:8)

Help me to fill my years on earth, O Holy Spirit, with works pleasing to You.

Living a Braveheart Life

Randall Wallace wrote the screenplay for the Academy Award-winning film "Braveheart," about William Wallace and the fight for Scottish independence. But he's also had some personal examples of living courageously.

During a "Christopher Closeup" interview about his book "Living the Braveheart Life," he cited two of his college professors, Hilda and Mikhail Pavlov. The Pavlovs survived the siege of Leningrad during World War II, along with other hardships, so Wallace was surprised they lived with such vibrancy.

He asked Mrs. Pavlov if she had been able to take anything with her when she left Russia. She said, "Three times in my life, I have been somewhere where someone ran into the room and said, 'If you don't get up and run that way right now, you'll die.' I could take nothing with me. I have no regrets."

Wallace said, "It caused me to think about what we consider the necessary stuff in our lives — I need this or that to be happy. But she had gone through the crucible of knowing that those things were unnecessary, that what made a life was love."

Be strong and of good courage.
(2 Chronicles 32:7)

Teach me what I need to be happy, Holy Spirit.

Generation Hope

In Malawi, Africa, in 2002, Magnus MacFarlane-Barrow founded the organization Mary's Meals to feed 200 hungry children. In 2016, a movie about his work—titled "Generation Hope"—was shown at France's Cannes Film Festival.

MacFarlane-Barrow revealed that, thanks to the support of generous donors, Mary's Meals now feeds one million hungry and impoverished children a day: "Children who used to miss school are now in classrooms, children who were once too hungry to concentrate can now learn...and parents who were tortured by not being able to feed their children every day have more peace.

"And now, at this point in our growth, we see that a beautiful revolution is taking place as a new generation, once fed by Mary's Meals, begins to find its voice. We call them 'Generation Hope.' This is what this film is about—the university students, singers, farmers, teachers, DJs, footballers, and a myriad of other happy young people who, well-nourished and well-educated, are now finding their own way in life."

If you offer your food to the hungry...then your light shall rise in the darkness. (Isaiah 58:10)

May I be a source of hope to all generations, Holy Spirit.

The Mother of all Orphans

Sindhutai Sapkal has endured a great deal of hardship in her 68 years of life. Born in a small village in India, she was married at the age of 10 to a man 20 years her senior. Sapkal's husband was physically and emotionally abusive. Ten years after their marriage, he turned his young wife from their home; she was then nine months pregnant with their first child.

Rejected by her husband and even her own mother, Sapkal was tempted to give up on life right then and there. However, concern for her daughter led her to the streets to beg for what she never received from her own family. Her journey for survival introduced her to countless orphaned children in need of food, shelter and above all, the unconditional love of a mother.

Sapkal became this mother to many of these children: over 1,400 of them to be exact. This gave rise to her well-earned nickname the "mother of orphans." To date, she has received over 500 awards for her tireless work with these children, but all the money she receives goes towards creating homes for her growing family. What a rich example of motherhood to emulate!

Then the mother of the child says..."I will not leave without you." (2 Kings 4:30)

Father, bless all mothers, and guide them in Your ways.

Encourage! Encourage! Encourage!

Have you ever been in the position of wanting to offer a word of encouragement to somebody who seemed to need it, but let the opportunity slip by?

You're not alone. And that's too bad. An encouraging remark can make someone's day. Occasionally it can even change a life—and a world.

Dr. Dale Turner tells how Alexander Graham Bell described his theory of telegraphing speech to the director of the Smithsonian Institute. Bell concluded by confessing that he didn't have enough knowledge of electricity to develop and test his theory.

His enthusiastic colleague urged him, "Well then, get it!" Bell did. And we, in time, got the benefit of his inventive genius with the development of the telephone.

So, next time, don't hesitate, speak up. In large ways or small, your encouragement matters.

Consider how to provoke one another to love and good deeds...encouraging one another. (Hebrews 10:24-25)

Holy Spirit, show me how to "provoke" and encourage others to good works!

News Anchor's Guide to Life

Emmy Award-winning news anchor Ernie Anastos won the 2016 Christopher Life Achievement Award for his professional achievement, dedication to various charities, and exemplary character, grounded in his love of God and family. During his acceptance speech, he shared a poem he wrote called "Life." It contains words of wisdom for everyone:

"There comes a time in life when we won't be so concerned about minutes, hours, or days. Things we've collected we'll probably give to others. Money, fame and power also become irrelevant. Wins and losses that once seemed important don't matter. Even grudges and resentments disappear.

"So what really matters? The value of your life is seen in every act of integrity, compassion, or sacrifice that enriches and encourages others. It's about character. Not just what you have learned, but what you have taught. More than what you got, it's what you gave. Remember, life is really measured not by success, but by significance."

Whoever wishes to become great among you must be your servant. (Mark 10:43)

Build up my character so I can be more like You, Jesus.

A Texan's New York Adventure

Sometimes, it takes a Texan to finish off what a New Yorker began. Police Chief Sean Ford of Sunset Valley, Texas, was in New York with his family on vacation last year when he saw two men scuffling on Fifth Avenue. Police later said that one of the men, Roman Mercado, had stolen perfume valued at $118 from the Abercrombie & Fitch store. The other man was a security guard trying to stop him.

Ford told his family members to call 911 and then stopped the fight, according to an account in the *New York Post*. He identified himself as a police officer and then quickly determined details of the event, holding Mercado until the NYPD showed up. They thanked him for getting involved, and an appreciative Ford praised the New York police for their professionalism.

Chief Ford had been to Manhattan before; he came there after the 9/11 attacks with a team from Texas. "I have a lot of respect for the NYPD ever since," he said.

Trust in the Lord, and do good; so you will live in the land, and enjoy security. (Psalm 37:3)

Thank You, heavenly Father, for the presence of those who act with integrity to safeguard Your people.

The Laredo Samaritans

They call themselves the Samaritans. They dress alike (in pink shirts), they work and they pray together, all to fulfill the message emblazoned on the backs of their shirts: "Whatever you do for the least of My brothers, you do unto Me."

This quote comes from Matthew 25:40, and it describes what the Samaritans are all about. Their mission is to lend a hand to anyone who needs it—the elderly, the disabled, the sick, the lonely and the grieving. The group of 10 women is from San Javier Mission in Laredo, Texas, and they were founded three years ago by their pastor, Father Bill Davis.

They were written up in *Catholic News Service,* with an acknowledgment to their sponsoring organization, the Catholic Extension Society. They do a number of things: clean houses, visit people, comfort in times of disaster, and pray the rosary. In short, they make life better for everyone, one person at a time.

One woman helped by the Samaritans now goes to church, which she hadn't done before. "We cry, we pray, we sing together. It is so powerful," the Samaritans exclaim.

Who is my neighbor? (Luke 10:29)

How can I lend someone a helping hand today, Jesus?

Sanctuary from Stress — and Much More

Rabbi Abraham Joshua Heschel called the Sabbath "a sanctuary in time." In an age when we rush to cram as much activity as possible into every minute, it's especially important to take and make a time of refuge from constant "doing," to have a time for "being."

A Sabbath rest gives us time to spend on our relationship with our family and friends, and our God. It gives us time for ourselves. The sanctuary of the Sabbath is the day on which we allow ourselves to accomplish nothing. It is a day for silence and music, conversation and reading, walking slowly and playing games, and especially for prayer and meditation.

A day of "sanctuary" gives us rest emotionally as well as physically; frees us from preoccupations that separate us from God's healing presence; renews us with peace that only God can give; prevents stress from damaging our health; and gives us a taste of the eternal rest promised to us.

Ought not this woman, a daughter of Abraham whom Satan bound for eighteen long years, be set free from this bondage on the Sabbath day? (Luke 13:16)

Liberate me, Lord, so that I can enter into Your rest.

Grace in the Thrift Store

Laura Yeager was browsing through her local thrift store when she started chatting with a stranger. She discovered that this woman's name was Vilma and she was from Colombia. Before parting ways, Vilma said to Laura, "Pray for me." Since Laura was religious, she was happy to do so.

Then, Laura asked Vilma, "Would you pray for me, too? I have breast cancer." Vilma revealed that she had survived breast cancer herself in 2005. Not only did she offer to pray for Laura, but to pray over her. Right there in the store. Laura remembers Vilma saying "Dear Jesus, we pray that you heal Laura's cancer." The whole experience moved Laura to tears.

Recalling the incident on the website Aleteia, Laura concluded, "What happened in the thrift store was the most spontaneous religious experience I'd ever had. I praise God that He appears to us when we need Him most. He appeared to me in the form of a Colombian lady with similar taste to mine in a thrift store in Cuyahoga Falls, Ohio, in the middle of May of 2016. There, I was gifted with God's grace."

Pray for one another, so that you may be healed. (James 5:16)

Guide me in forging lasting spiritual friendships, Savior.

Babysitting Money Changes Lives

After graduating from high school in 2005, New Jersey's Maggie Doyne opted to be a globe trekker for a year. It was her trip to Nepal that ended up changing the course of her life.

As reported by the website A Mighty Girl, Doyne saw the devastating effects that the Nepalese Civil War had on the country's children. She contacted her parents and asked them to wire her all the money she had saved from years of babysitting: $5,000. She then used those funds to open an orphanage.

By 2015, Doyne's dream had expanded beyond anything she had imagined. She is now the mother and legal guardian of close to 50 children, and she's helped build a community school, medical clinic, and organic food garden. Her work earned her the CNN Hero of the Year Award.

One of the keys to Doyne's success is listening to the needs of her Nepalese neighbors before starting any project. She says, "It's become so much more than just a little girl with a backpack and a big dream. It's become a community....[I] hope this sets a precedent for what our world can be and look like."

The wise woman builds her house.
(Proverbs 14:1)

May I use my talents to build up love and community, Lord.

If You're Not Part of the Solution...

David Oyelowo's acting career may take up a lot of his time, but he remains a man who is grounded in his Christian faith and is willing to share it with others. As such, he and his wife run a youth group at their church because he realizes these young people need God in order to deal with the negative cultural influences all around them.

During a "Christopher Closeup" interview, Oyelowo said, "I think the challenges young people face are greater now than when I was a teenager [because of] social media and just how much we are bombarded from every side by images of pornography or drugs or just morally questionable things.

"'Sex sells' has gone on to become a religion—and that's a challenging thing for young people, especially those who are trying to stay pure [and not] ruin their lives by getting into all kinds of different things that would and could do that. So my belief is: if you're not part of the solution, you're part of the problem. I've been afforded this platform, which hopefully can oxidize some of that, so you just try and do your part."

They are to teach what is good. (Titus 2:3)

Lead me in being a problem solver, Divine Wisdom.

Thank God Each Day

The late writer William Arthur Ward had some thought-provoking ideas on prayer you might consider:

"Wonderful things happen to us when we live expectantly, believe confidently, and pray affirmatively.

"Seeking to find how I should pray, this came to mind: Thank God each day.

"Prayer does not always bring us what we want; rather it helps us to become the kind of persons we should be.

"The value of prayer is not in what it gives us, but in what it makes us.

"It is not primarily a method of getting, but it is a splendid way of growing."

In one translation of Luke's Gospel, Jesus is said to have spent a night "in communion with God." "Communion," is a definition of prayer from the heart, with the heart, to the heart of God. Pray today.

Your servant has found courage to pray this prayer to You. (2 Samuel 7:27)

Jesus, teach me to integrate prayer into my daily life.

Testing the Unknown

Many jobs entail risk, but one that seems almost synonymous with danger is that of test pilots. Their job is to check and evaluate the safety, operation and durability of an aircraft that's never been flown before. They must be on guard at all times, and attentive to the slightest detail.

It's a demanding job that requires confidence and bravery because no matter how carefully test flights are planned, there is always the element of the unknown.

Truly, there is an element of risk and uncertainty in every new venture. Don't be afraid to step into the unknown simply because it is unknown. Progress always entails risk. Plan ahead intelligently and have courage.

For God all things are possible. (Mark 10:27)

Remind me, Redeemer, that indeed all things are possible with You at my side.

The Footprints of Jesus

When Deacon Greg Kandra traveled to the Holy Land with a tour group, they saw a stone that legend says holds the final footprint of Jesus before He ascended into heaven. While others claimed to see a faint outline, Deacon Kandra didn't see anything. He wondered if his faith was too weak, but later came upon a new perspective.

Deacon Kandra wrote on his Aleteia blog: "I've come to realize that the most enduring footprints of Christ are not to be found on a pebbled hilltop in the Middle East...They are the footprints He has left on lives. And they are everywhere...You will find them in New York City, at the Catholic Worker, where volunteers ladle soup every day to dozens of homeless men and women. His footprints are there, in the soup line.

"You will find them on the floors of nurseries where mothers walk all night caring for their sick infants, and on the coffee-stained carpets of church basements, where weekly AA meetings are held...Look carefully. You might even find them in your own living room."

Whoever has seen Me has seen the Father. (John 14:9)

Help me to see Your presence in every aspect of my daily life, Son of God.

Devotion, Part One

Jesse Brown grew up dirt poor in Mississippi, the son of a deacon and a missionary. As a child, he fell in love with the idea of being a Navy pilot, even though that was an impossible dream for African-Americans at that time.

Tom Hudner, meanwhile, was a white New Englander raised in a well-to-do family. One of the main lessons his father taught him was, "A man will reveal himself through his character, not his skin color." Hudner went on to join the Navy when the U.S. was in the midst of World War II because he wanted to help. Brown managed to defy the odds and enter the Navy as well, despite racism still being rampant in the U.S.

Adam Makos, author of a biography about Brown and Hudner called "Devotion," credits Brown's Christianity with his approach. During a "Christopher Closeup" interview, Makos said, "[Jesse] saw what America could be, and he knew he loved the spirit of this country. I think that faith was his anchor. It gave him that promise that things can be better."

More of the story tomorrow.

[Men] look on the outward appearance, but the Lord looks on the heart. (1 Samuel 16:7)

May my faith guide me to treat everyone equally, Creator.

Devotion, Part Two

Though Jesse Brown had faced discrimination throughout his life, his experience in the Navy during the Korean War actually broke down racial barriers, as it did for many people of different ethnicities and religions.

During a "Christopher Closeup" interview, "Devotion" author Adam Makos explained, "[Everyone fighting] knows that their lives are all intertwined, so true value shines through at that time, true character. Hatred and things like racism, they go right out the window, because we really have to rely on each other. So I think those men came home from that war, and they were changed forever in their attitudes about other races. It was more or less the civilians in the United States who carried on that legacy of racism for the next 30 years."

Superficial differences sure didn't matter to Hudner and Brown, who became good friends. And one fateful day during a mission over dangerous North Korean territory, Hudner demonstrated the lengths to which he would go out of devotion to his fellow aviator. More of the story tomorrow.

The same Lord is Lord of all. (Romans 10:12)

Help me to reexamine any prejudices I hold in my heart, Lord.

Devotion, Part Three

Everything changed for Navy pilots Tom Hudner and Jesse Brown on December 4, 1950. Historian Adam Makos explained, "The Korean War had turned dire. We had 10,000 U.S. Marines surrounded by 100,000 Chinese communist troops at a place called the Chosin Reservoir, in northern North Korea. Men like Tom and Jesse would fly [from their nearby naval carrier ships] to give air support to the Marines. They would drop bombs and strafe, and that's when Jesse Brown was shot down. He was hit by a bullet from the ground, and he crash-landed in the only place he could: on the side of a North Korean mountain."

Hudner was Brown's wingman, and he saw smoke rising from the nose of Jesse's plane, which lay 13 miles behind enemy lines. Hudner said, "I'm going in."

Makos continued, "Tom knew his friend was about to die, and he was willing to give his own life to try to change that. With his wheels up, Tom circled around and came to a skidding, screeching stop alongside of Jesse's plane."

The conclusion of the story tomorrow.

The righteous are as bold as a lion. (Proverbs 28:1)

Instill me with the devotion and courage to help friends in trouble, Lord.

Devotion, Part Four

After Tom Hudner got out of his plane, he stepped into the deep snow of the North Korean winter and tried to save Jesse Brown's life. Hudner put out the fire from Brown's plane with his bare hands. Unfortunately, the pioneering African-American pilot was so badly injured that he died. His one comfort was that he wasn't alone at the end—a fact that also brought some solace to Brown's widow, Daisy.

Hudner survived and received the Medal of Honor for his actions. His ship's captain said, "There has been no finer act of unselfish heroism in military history." Despite these accolades, this story was never widely told until "Devotion" author Adam Makos discovered it and wrote about it after recently meeting Hudner.

He believes that more attention should be paid to the history of the Korean War and he hopes his book piques interest: "This beautiful story can open our eyes to these forgotten heroes [so] no generation of American veterans will be forgotten."

I will not fail you or forsake you. (Joshua 1:5)

Welcome the souls of those killed in war into Your loving arms, Prince of Peace.

A Leap of Faith

A day after she survived an apartment fire by jumping three stories into the arms of waiting police officers, nine-year-old Sofiya Doroshenko was as relaxed as any other schoolgirl. Still, she clearly remembered the incident. "I was scared," she said.

Sofiya, who recently came to this country from Ukraine, lives with her parents, both medical professionals, in Mahwah, New Jersey. Her mother had just left for work and her father was due home any minute when the fire broke out in the third-floor apartment across from theirs.

Her parents had told her to "trust the police" in this country, and she did just that when flames trapped her on her balcony. Sofiya leapt into the enjoined arms of Lt. Jeffrey Dino, Sgt. Brendan Mullin and Officer Thomas Solimano.

Marina Villenueve, writing for *The Record* of Hackensack, interviewed the girl's parents in the motel where they stayed. Sofiya's mother Yuliya expressed gratitude for the community's generosity and donations.

Then they cried out to the Lord in their trouble, and He saved them from their distress. (Psalm 107:13)

Saving Lord, may I always put my trust in You.

A Beautiful Ministry

Carol Welsh is retiring from a "beautiful ministry" after 17 years as head of the Parish Nursing program at St. Joseph's Church in Nashville, Tennessee. But she's leaving behind a number of volunteers who'll carry on her noble legacy.

According to a story by Ned Andrew Solomon in the *Tennessee Register,* the program allows registered nurses to care for individuals while promoting health and wellness in the surrounding community as well. At St. Joseph's, Welsh headed a team of 20 to 25 nurse volunteers and lay parishioners.

"The parish nurse is a representative, first and foremost, of her parish, her church. So you've got to be grounded in your spirituality," she said.

Mary Donnelly, who coordinates the training program at St. Thomas Hospital, added that all parish nurses are "trusted professionals who bridge the gap between the congregation and the health care system."

I pray that...you may be strengthened in your inner being with power through His Spirit. (Ephesians 3:16)

Holy Spirit, fill me with the strength to answer Your call wherever my life and career take me.

Lesson from a June Bug

A Christopher friend named Martha was on a silent retreat at Saint Emma Retreat House in Greensburg, Pennsylvania, taking part in Eucharistic Adoration when a June bug came flying at her head. "I swatted it with my hand," wrote Martha in a letter to us. "It landed on its back on the pew in front of me. It was moving around on its back with six or more legs, struggling to right itself to its feet."

Martha's attention returned to the Eucharist, but her eyes were eventually drawn back to the June bug, which had righted itself and was slowly moving on.

At this point, she felt like God spoke a message to her, saying: "Martha, for many years you were like this June bug. You struggled and were not able to move forward. However, when you started to focus on Me, you were, through My grace, able to right yourself and make progress."

Martha took this unique experience as a sign that she was on the right road after some struggles in the past.

I keep the Lord always before me. (Psalm 16:8)

Life's struggles can be distracting, Jesus. When my attention wanders, draw me back to You.

Coat of Many Colors

Growing up in the Smoky Mountains of Tennessee, Dolly Parton's family had a lot of love and a lot of kids, but not a lot of money. However, those times inspired Parton's songwriting, including her favorite song, "Coat of Many Colors." The lyrics recall her mom using old rags to make her a coat, just like Joseph wore in the Bible.

In 2015, Parton joined forces with her friend Sam Haskell to produce a TV movie based on that song. Not only did audiences give the movie high ratings for its faith-and-family-friendly appeal, we gave it a Christopher Award. Haskell attributes that faith dimension with the project's success.

During a "Christopher Closeup" interview, he said, "It's something that I don't think people are getting enough of today, when dealing with socioeconomic and political times that are unsettling. To find something faith-filled, I think, is what brought the audience to us. People were anxious to see something they could hold onto at a time when they really needed it."

Trust in the Lord with all your heart. (Proverbs 3:5)

Though my heart and mind are often filled with anxiety, Jesus, increase my faith so that I find peace.

What Women Want in a Husband

If you're a man looking to get married, Monica Gabriel has some advice for you. As the Relationships Editor for *Verily* magazine, she's discovered that two of the primary qualities women are looking for in a husband are confidence and humility.

During a "Christopher Closeup" interview, Gabriel elaborated on both: "For confidence, women want a man who's sure of his direction, who'll be a leader, who knows himself. This means that this is a man that she can trust, and I think these days that man is hard to find. Women are used to meeting men who are unsure of themselves, who are not leaders, especially not leaders in relationships.

"Humility is closely tied to that because it is an essential characteristic in a leader. It's also someone a woman can be vulnerable with. A humble man is a man of faith, usually. He's a man that leans on God for his strength. A man who is humble, who turns to God when he needs strength, is a man who will move mountains for her, for their relationship, for their family."

He who loves his wife loves himself. (Ephesians 5:28)

Jesus, help all people looking for a spouse to grow in virtue themselves, and to reflect Your love to others.

The Holy Spirit is an Artist

When Kathleen Hattrup first got to know her husband, who was an artist and painter, she marveled at how he seemed to get so many elements wrong as he started a picture. But when she revisited the painting after a while, she discovered that "those seemingly false additions were perfectly intentional and designed to cast the shadow just here or give light just there."

That long-ago lesson gave Hattrup some spiritual insight that she recently conveyed to her five-year-old daughter, who also displays artistic tendencies. Prior to Pentecost, Hattrup said to the girl, "I know why you and the Holy Spirit are great friends." The girl asked, "Why?"

As she recalled on the website Aleteia, Hattrup responded, "Because He's an artist like you. He's living in your soul and He's making it look like Jesus. And if you ever do something that isn't like Jesus, it's like coloring in the wrong spot, or spilling a bunch of paint. But the Holy Spirit comes along and erases it, and if He can't get it all erased, then He uses the stain and makes it become part of His picture."

**The Spirit helps us in our weakness.
(Romans 8:26)**

Create beauty in my soul, Holy Spirit.

Maintaining Healthy Pregnancies in Congo

Getting pregnant in the Democratic Republic of Congo can be a risky business. The African nation has one of the highest maternal and infant mortality rates in the world. So when Gisele Biringanine discovered she was expecting, she panicked. Her first two pregnancies had ended in miscarriage.

But this pregnancy would be different thanks to support from Catholic Relief Services. As described by Michael Stulman in the CRS publication *The Wooden Bell,* Biringanine had access to free prenatal care and regular support from health volunteers in the community. She also received assistance during childbirth at the community health clinic, where she gave birth to a beautiful baby boy. Both she and her schoolteacher-husband were delighted.

"Women used to deliver at home," she said with a deep measure of gratitude. "Now we know to go to the health center before the baby arrives." For many, that's a life-saving decision.

They shall not labor in vain...for they shall be offspring blessed by the Lord. (Isaiah 65:23)

Father of mercy, protect and bless mothers and their children everywhere.

A Routine Day Turns Dangerous

It had started off as a routine day for Jay Moss. After a workout at the gym, he would head to his job in Clifton, New Jersey, as sales manager for an educational software company. But then came a frantic plea for help: a woman had driven her car into the Passaic River near the gym. The man asking for help saw the accident, but said he couldn't swim. There was only one thing to do—and Moss did it.

As Jim Norman and Stefanie Dazio reported in *The Record* of Hackensack, Moss stripped to his gym shorts and plunged into the river. When he got to the car it was in about 10 feet of water, which was rising inside. "I could see a woman inside floating in the water," he recalled. "She was unconscious."

Moss finally opened the car door and carried the woman to safety, first swimming and then, when the water was shallower, walking to shore. "You never know what's coming or how you will react," he said later. "You just gotta do the right thing."

He reached down from on high...He drew me out of mighty waters. He delivered me. (Psalm 18:16-17)

I give You thanks, Savior, for all those You have sent to deliver me when I was in trouble.

Recovering Addict Finds Hope in Bible

As a recovering alcoholic and drug addict, Scott Weeman found comfort in studying the Bible. As he explained during a "Christopher Closeup" interview about his website CatholicInRecovery.com: "I familiarized myself with those who God called in the Old Testament. I learned about Paul's conversion from one who persecuted Christians to one who brought the Christian life to new worlds. I found that one need not be a holy, devout person for God to call them to do good.

"And then, getting to know the saints brought us to another level. They were real-life examples of people who have turned their lives around and found that their struggle brought about humility and a sense of devout care for others and for the Lord."

Weeman also found healing through his community of recovering addicts: "I'm offered a daily reprieve based on the maintenance of my spiritual condition. And I can only maintain my spiritual condition through prayer and community."

[God] saved us...not according to our works but according to His own purpose and grace. (2 Timothy 1:9)

Regardless of my past, lead me to a holy future, Father.

The Hutto Project

Create a children's choir in a refugee camp. That became the goal of Kate Eberstadt when she heard from a friend working at a camp in Germany. The children there had already endured tragic circumstances, so Eberstadt wanted to introduce the healing and unifying gift of music into their lives.

As reported by Mic.com, the American college graduate named her effort after a teacher who had encouraged her own gift for music. It's called The Hutto Project, and its motto is, "Spread Light."

The choir includes 27 children between the ages of three and 21, who speak languages including Arabic, Farsi, Russian, and more. They will create an original composition to perform at a concert in Berlin.

Eberstadt said, "While this international humanitarian tragedy has adopted political implications, there is nothing political about a child's need for both structure and self-expression. Our program intends to honor both of these needs for children who have been forced to grow up very quickly."

He put a new song in my mouth, a song of praise to our God. (Psalm 40:3)

Unite the people of the world in peace, Divine Savior.

Love Doesn't Die, Part One

In 1950, at age 22, Jean Rolf gave birth to Susan, the first of her five children. The doctor soon told her that Susan was "a Mongoloid," the term that was used before Dr. Down found the extra chromosome that caused the condition.

Jean and her husband were ordered to place the girl in a state institution and tell everyone she died—and the hospital wouldn't release Susan until they found a facility.

Jean was horrified because she believed that Susan was a gift from God. With help from her husband's brother, Father Raymond Rolf, they convinced the hospital to let them take Susan home with the promise they would put her in a home run by nuns when she was five years old.

That was a promise they never followed through on, though, because Susan bonded with her parents—and their love for her grew stronger every day. While Susan faced challenges, they learned that she was far more capable of living a fulfilling life than society or the medical establishment believed.

You knit me together in my mother's womb. (Psalm 139:13)

Help us to see all children as a gift from God, Creator.

Love Doesn't Die, Part Two

Jean Rolf, her husband, and the rest of their children built a beautiful life together. While schooling for children with Down Syndrome didn't exist in the 1950s, Jean taught Susan a lot, and she was considered high-functioning. The one thing that came naturally to Susan was showing love and compassion to others.

In 1995, Jean, now a widow, began having some health issues and worried that she might not be around to take care of Susan. She, therefore, placed her in a good facility for people with Down Syndrome, where she made friends with the other residents. As fate would have it, Susan passed away first, but her mother remembers her special child every day.

In a letter to The Christophers, Jean recalled, "At her funeral, her four siblings stood up at church and said how they learned unconditional love from [Susan]. I continue to miss my husband and Susan, but am thankful for the wonderful years we had together. And I believe, 'Love doesn't die.' I feel their love and expect to be reunited with them in Heaven."

God is love, and those who abide in love abide in God, and God abides in them. (1 John 4:16)

May I choose to live in Your eternal love, Father.

Bullied Girl Finds Welcome

"Go back to your country, you Nazi." Those were the words that awaited 12-year-old Cecilia Worosch when she arrived in the U.S. in 1952. Her classmates knew that she had immigrated from Germany and spoke German, so they judged her on that basis.

It didn't matter to them that she and her family were originally from Yugoslavia, and that they had spent two years as prisoners in a Russian concentration camp despite the fact that they had nothing to do with the Nazis. They eventually escaped to Germany, where they lived a few years before moving to New York to pursue a better life.

Several years later, Cecilia applied for a job at the store Bergdorf Goodman. "Miss Jeri," her prospective boss who conducted the interview, was Jewish, so Cecilia told her about her family history and about being bullied in school. She was afraid her German background might cause a problem.

Miss Jeri told Cecilia that her own parents were Russian Jews who escaped persecution, so she would face no bias from her. Cecilia got hired and found a friend and mentor in Miss Jeri, who finally made this young woman feel welcome in her new country.

Come in, my daughter, and welcome. (Tobit 11:17)

Help me be welcoming to strangers, Messiah.

A Christ-Like Life

College sophomore Valeria Tkacik is a Mother Teresa Scholar at Ave Maria University in Naples, Florida. She has served on her student government, is an extremely skilled lacrosse player, and enjoys playing basketball, golf, track and soccer. Her active lifestyle is somewhat surprising because she performs every task with only one arm.

Originally from Russia, Tkacik was born with *congenital shoulder disarticulation,* a medical condition which means she has no left arm. However, neither Tkacik nor her adoptive parents allowed her disability to affect her quality of life. "My parents always believed they would never set any limitations on me," Tkacik tells *Catholic News Service's* Diane Xavier. "They always encouraged me to do my best."

"Even though I only have one arm, God has given me so many other beautiful gifts," she concludes. "It's been [an] honor and blessing to please the Lord with all the events and activities I've been doing...Actions speak louder than words, and I just love my life. My goal is to continue to live a Christ-like life."

I praise You, for I am...wonderfully made. (Psalm 139:14)

God, may our actions always reflect the depth of our faith.

The Seven-Step Prayer Process

In "The Four Signs of a Dynamic Catholic," Matthew Kelly suggests we practice a seven-step daily Prayer Process:

- **"Gratitude:** Begin by thanking God...for whatever you are most grateful today.
- **"Awareness:** Revisit the times of the past 24 hours when you were and were not the best version of yourself. Talk to God about these situations and what you learned from them.
- **"Significant Moments:** Identify something you experienced today and explore what God might be trying to say to you.
- **"Peace:** Ask God to forgive you for any wrong you have committed and to fill you with a deep and abiding peace.
- **"Freedom:** Speak with God about how He is inviting you to change your life, so that you can experience the freedom to be the best version of yourself.
- **"Others:** Lift up to God anyone you feel called to pray for today, asking God to bless and guide them.
- **"Prayer:** Finish by praying the Our Father."

**I have heard your prayer and your plea.
(1 Kings 9:3)**

I yearn to grow closer to You in prayer, Lord. Send me Your Holy Spirit to guide my way.

Diverting the Floodwaters

The floodwaters of the Mississippi River reached as far south as Vicksburg last winter. But, thanks in part to senior class members at St. Aloysius High School, no serious flooding took place.

A report by Mary Margaret Halford in the *Mississippi Catholic* detailed the work of the teens, who gave up some of their free time to load sandbags in downtown Vicksburg to help divert the flood.

The seniors (accompanied by a group of alumni) chose to forgo their own afternoon plans to join city workers near the waterfront to do some hands-on work, shoveling sand into bags to fortify the city's defenses.

"The kids were excited to do something that they knew would have an immediate impact on their city," said Joan Thornton, theology teacher at the school. "They were happy to do it. They really understand that the river is part of who we are in Vicksburg."

Many waters cannot quench love, neither can floods drown it. (Song of Solomon 8:7)

In the storms of life, Lord, let me show love in action.

The Wonder of Your Heart

"I cannot understand how any thinking person can deny there is a Supreme Being [behind] all of this creation." This thought dominated a letter sent to us by an eighty-two-year-old Ohio doctor.

"Take my heart for instance," he continued. "It beats 72 times a minute—4,320 times an hour—103,680 times a day—37,843,200 times a year—3,103,142,400 times in 82 years, and still keeps beating day and night."

It is so easy for us to take for granted not only the constant beat of our hearts, but the innumerable wonders of creation. Pause from time to time and reflect prayerfully on them in the spirit of the Hebrew Psalmist, who joyfully proclaimed:

When I look at Your heavens, the work of Your fingers, the moon and the stars that You have established; what are human beings that You are mindful of them, mortals that You care for them? Yet You have made them a little lower than God, and crowned them with glory and honor. (Psalm 8:3-5)

May I show by my words and deeds, Holy Spirit, that I truly reflect Your glory in all that I say and do.

Dads and Education Change Everything

Pakistani teenager Malala Yousafzi, a Nobel laureate, truly appreciates the value of education, particularly for girls in the developing world. She literally put her life on the line for it.

Film director Davis Guggenheim wanted to capture Malala's extraordinary bravery in his movie "He Named Me Malala." He was inspired after the girl survived an assassination attempt by the Taliban, but he wanted another angle for his film as well. He told *AM/New York* that he found it in her father Ziauddin. "I realized that there was something really interesting about the father-daughter relationship."

Today, a few years after her attack, Malala still suffers some residual effects from her injuries, but they haven't slowed her down much. She continues to advocate for girls' education.

It makes a big difference when parents support the education of their children. For girls in many families across the world, the support of their fathers can often change everything.

Let the wise also hear and gain in learning, and the discerning acquire skill. (Proverbs 1:5)

Help fathers, Jesus, appreciate their importance in the lives of their children.

'A Light No Dark Could Ever Steal'

In 2015, when a white gunman shot and killed nine African-Americans attending a prayer group in a South Carolina church, singer-songwriter Sarah Hart felt "crushed" by this act of racial hatred. In response, she wrote a song called "Hallowed Ground," which she put on her album "Til the Song is Sung."

It includes the lyrics, "There is holiness in every crack and scar / And what we've rent upon this earth You mean to heal / So until my bones return into the dust / Let me be a light no dark could ever steal."

The lyrics serve as a call to action for herself and anyone listening. During a "Christopher Closeup" interview, Hart said, "For me, the commitment is to be gentle, to be loving, to be kind, to embody as best as I can, the gifts of the Holy Spirit to the world. I wept as I wrote that song because that's my prayer: to walk humbly on this planet with God and try to give that example so that others may do the same thing."

What does the Lord require of you but to do justice, and to love kindness, and to walk humbly with your God? (Micah 6:8)

In this world of divisions, Lord, help me to serve as a beacon of peace.

Kelly Clarkson Encourages Fathers

A seven-months-pregnant Kelly Clarkson served as a guest judge on "American Idol" in 2016, and also sung an original song called "Piece by Piece." It was inspired by Clarkson's father abandoning her family when she was young, and the damage his absence temporarily had on her self-worth. But the song also takes a more positive spin when Clarkson notes that her own husband is a devoted dad to their children.

In an interview with the *Associated Press*, Clarkson revealed how her daughter's birth affected her perspective on the importance of fatherhood: "When you hold this little human you've created, now I think I understand the depth of the loss I had not having a father figure growing up."

Clarkson added that while she doesn't have a relationship with her father, "I'm in a very forgiving place about it and everybody's human. But I get choked up because I realize how lucky I am...A lot of girls that grew up with their daddy issues and not having that figure in their life, [they] take a very different road. I feel lucky that I'm not that girl."

Fathers make known to children your faithfulness. (Isaiah 38:19)

Inspire all fathers to be devoted to their children, Lord.

Bringing Medicine and Encouragement

When Chicago doctor Kevin Hunt co-founded the charity Medical Aid to Northern Uganda (MANU) in 2007, his aim was to update the equipment at the main hospital there, which dated back to the 1950s. Through donations, that goal was accomplished, so now they're working on building a new emergency room and triage center.

Dr. Hunt's effect on Northern Ugandans, specifically in the Diocese of Lira, goes beyond providing supplies and medicines, though. The presence of MANU team members during their mission trips makes a lasting impression as well.

During a "Christopher Closeup" interview, Dr. Hunt said, "You feel like you're giving back and the people are responding to it—even to small things [such as] touching people or reassuring them or even looking into their eyes. They have a better outlook on things because we give them encouragement."

He concludes, "You have to reach out to every person—the lowest person or the highest person in the world. We all are human beings, and you have to treat people equally."

Bear one another's burdens, and...fulfill the law of Christ. (Galatians 6:2)

Let me be a source of comfort to someone in need, Lord.

Dream, Believe, Do, Repeat

Singer-songwriter Audrey Assad learned a valuable lesson from her Syrian refugee father growing up: "Dream, believe, do, repeat." That was the approach he practiced when he moved to the United States in 1973, with his two siblings and mother.

In an interview with Aleteia's Zoe Romanowsky for World Refugee Day, Audrey recalled, "My father, Roy Assad, was a sponsored child through a church program in Syria, and the man who had been sending money every month in my dad's name was one of their only contacts here [in the U.S.]. He eventually employed my dad and gave him his start in the insurance business, in which my father still works over 40 years later...

"My dad has worked tooth and nail to accomplish his dreams and goals—as an immigrant with no college education, he has owned companies ranging from insurance agencies to restaurants. I've watched him dig his hands into every city in which he's lived...He isn't satisfied with simply residing somewhere—he's driven to make it a better place for everyone."

Go from your country...to the land that I will show you. I will make of you a great nation. (Genesis 12:1-2)

Guide refugees toward creating productive lives, Jesus.

Tiny Hole Empties Reservoir

A tiny hole in a 400-foot-dam was the undoing of a 30 million gallon reservoir in New Jersey many years ago. Although the small leak seemed insignificant, it soon eroded into a gaping hole and threatened the collapse of the 123-year-old dam.

Many of the great problems of our age have their origins in defects which, like the little hole in the dam, are discounted as being of minor importance. But small acts of dishonesty, corruption, and subversion can be the beginnings of a deadly breakdown.

In today's fast-moving world, your continual vigilance is urgently needed. While avoiding extremes, be ever on the alert to detect the slightest flaws or faults which can spread, with a galloping speed, once they gain the upper hand.

What you, as one person, do—or fail to do—counts more than you think to promote God's truth.

Whoever brings back a sinner from wandering will save the sinner's soul from death and will cover a multitude of sins. (James 5:20)

Grant, O Lord, that I may always nurture the seeds of goodness in myself and others.

The Next Awful Week

One of Rebecca Frech's favorite summers with her children took place the year she first moved to her Texas community. As she wrote on her "Backwards in High Heels" blog, "New in town, and without social obligations, our days meandered their way through books, naps, and hanging out poolside. The cable was not yet on, and the internet had not yet captured their imaginations or sucked away their energy."

As summer 2016 approached, she longed for those simpler days and even considered suspending cable TV for the summer and changing all the internet passwords. Her kids were not excited by the idea. So Frech prayed and believes God sent help:

"In torrents of rain and flashes of lightning, our cable and internet went down...There is no way a repair man can get to us before the middle of next week. We're dark for seven days."

Secretly gleeful at the "horrified" faces of her children, Frech headed to the library. Her kids gave her a list of books they wanted to read, calling them their "life raft for the next awful week." For Frech, it didn't sound so awful after all.

His way is in whirlwind and storm. (Nahum 1:3)

Help me to enjoy life's simple pleasures, Creator.

Little Moments of Love

Country music star Brad Paisley sings a lot of romantic songs during his concerts, but one night in 2016, he played a role in what will hopefully be a lifelong romance.

As reported by People.com, Jason Smith brought his girlfriend Courtney Larger to a Paisley show in Phoenix, hoping to get close enough to the stage that he could get the singer's attention. Then, Smith would ask him if he could propose to Larger onstage. A security guard, however, hindered his plans, so Smith reached out to Paisley on Twitter, explaining the situation.

Paisley responded personally and invited Smith to a Nevada concert to make the proposal happen. Smith told Larger that they won free tickets to the show, so they made the five-hour trip. During the concert, Paisley invited the couple onstage, where Smith dropped to one knee and popped the question. Larger was so overwhelmed and surprised that she forgot to answer until Paisley reminded her. She said, "Yes."

Above all, maintain constant love for one another. (1 Peter 4:8)

Instill engaged couples with the love, wisdom, patience, and commitment required to make marriage work.

Who's Your Best Friend?

Norman Vincent Peale was a popular author and minister, but he started out as a reporter. The newsletter *Apple Seeds* reprinted a story about him (originally in *Leadership* magazine) about crossing paths with American industrialist Henry Ford.

"[Peale] asked Ford if he had any advice for a young man starting out in life. Ford responded, 'Who's your best friend, son?'

"Then before Peale could answer, Ford went on to say, 'I'll tell you who it is. It's the person who brings out the best in you. Always associate with the best people—that's where you will find such a person.'"

Years later, Peale affirmed the truth of that advice, saying, "A best friend is one who tells you, 'Yes, you can make your dreams come true. Yes, you have something valuable to offer to the world. Yes, your life can make a difference.'"

Peale also noted the importance of the opposite question: "Whose best friend are you?...When you answer [that question], make sure that you deserve that title by bringing out the best in that person, every day, in every way."

Encourage one another. (1 Thessalonians 5:11)

May I be a true friend to others, Divine Savior.

The Rural Life is a Good Life

What's the first thing you think of when you hear of a parish celebrating Rural Life Sunday? If you answered "farming," you'd be with the majority, but you just might be wrong, too.

According to Kay Keller—who, with her husband, Ron, formed the host couple for last year's celebration in Faribault, Minnesota—only about 10 percent of the enrollment at their parish, St. Michael's, Kenyon, are full-time farmers.

Ron, 56, is the fifth generation of Kellers to run his family farm. He and Kay have seven children, who help with its 154 acres. "A rural setting just means we live in a small community," Kay told Clare Kolars of *The Catholic Spirit*. "We're financially strong, but we always get a little nervous when there's talk of downsizing."

Her husband added some observations of his own about life in a small parish. "St. Michael's rural character consists of a close-knit community," said Ron, "where people are willing to help each other and celebrate together."

Judah and all its towns shall live there together, and the farmers and those who wander with their flocks. (Jeremiah 31:24)

Help me to be community-minded, Savior.

Hugh Jackman Finds God in Acting

Actor Hugh Jackman, known for starring in movies such as "X-Men" and "Les Misérables," brings a spiritual dimension to every job he does. As reported by *Parade* magazine, he was raised in a "very religious" Christian family, and still describes himself as a "religious person."

Jackman said, "In [the movie] 'Chariots of Fire,' the runner Eric Liddell says, 'When I run, I feel His pleasure.' And I feel that pleasure when I act and it's going well, particularly onstage. I feel what everyone's searching for, the feeling that unites us all. Call it 'God.'

"Before I go onstage every night, I pause and dedicate the performance to God, in the sense of 'Allow me to surrender.' When you allow yourself to surrender to the story, to the character, to the night, to the audience, transcendence happens. And when that happens, there is nothing like it on the planet. It's the moment people experience when they fall in love, which is equally frightening and exciting. That's what it feels like."

Humble yourselves before the Lord, and He will exalt you. (James 4:10)

Father, I surrender my will to You today.

Subway Clerk Saves the Day

Richard Singleton was on duty as a subway clerk, working in the token booth in the station at 28th Street and Park Avenue in Manhattan, when he observed two men arguing on the platform. It was when the fight escalated, and one of the two men menaced the other with a knife, that Singleton took action.

He promptly tackled the knife-wielder, a 27-year-old man, before he could slash the other combatant. The subway clerk had saved a man from serious injury or even death, and found himself being hailed as a hero.

"I think most New Yorkers will stand up and help each other," he told an interviewer from the *Daily News.*

"You never know how you'll react in that situation," he added. "New York is not perfect but we're here for each other. New York is a very diverse, multicultural city and state, and we come together in bad times and good."

Lawbreakers shrank back for fear of him; all the evildoers were confounded; and deliverance prospered at his hand. (1 Maccabees 3:6)

God of justice, strengthen me to stand up for others.

Flowers and Prayers

The year that South Dakota farmer Brian Barber planted sunflowers, he thought his crop was doomed by alternating periods of rain and drought. As the earth cracked, he noticed that the sunflowers grew roots that wandered this way and that until they found a crack in the soil.

Barber wanted to devote more time to God and prayer, but as a farmer he was either always busy or bone-tired. Until he learned to look for the cracks in his day.

In Barber's case, while doing his farming duties, he began to meditate on the Biblical parables that have to do with working the land. As a result, he said, he developed a connection with the Biblical farmers and with the God that made the harvest bountiful.

Like Brian Barber, you can incorporate more prayer into your own life, if you let your imagination guide you.

During those days He went out to the mountain to pray; and He spent the night in prayer to God. (Luke 6:12)

Lord, teach me to pray.

Score One for Determination

The record for most persistent golfer may have been set back in 1912 at the ladies' invitational at Shawnee-on-Delaware, Pennsylvania. In the qualifying round, a woman took 166 strokes to make the 130-yard sixteenth hole.

Her tee shot went right into the river and the ball floated downstream. She and her husband jumped into a rowboat and set out after the ball. They followed it a mile and a half before she was able to beach it. Then she had to play through the woods all the way back to the golf course.

This golfer's score may have been poor, but her determination was truly remarkable. When we do poorly at something we undertake, it's important not to become discouraged and give up. We can learn from our failure and do better next time.

Hear the word, hold it fast in an honest and good heart, and bear fruit with patient endurance. (Luke 8:15)

Though not every endeavor I undertake will be a success, Lord, grant me the patience and persistence to improve with each new effort.

Good Porches, Good Neighbors

"This world would be a better place if everyone had a front porch," said William Martin of Northport, New York, several years ago. The trend today is to build houses with a backyard and patio instead of the front porch that was popular years ago. True, a patio at the back of the house affords more privacy—maybe too much privacy.

Martin thought something important was lost, so he added a porch, and now calls it "one of the best moves we ever made."

The old-fashioned front porch was more than just a place to sit and relax, to enjoy the outdoors protected from sun and rain. It was a place that encouraged friendliness with neighbors. People walking by would smile and wave, often stopping to talk.

People need one another. Even the simple warmth of a friendly greeting can help lift our spirits.

Better is a neighbor who is nearby than kindred who are far away. (Proverbs 27:10)

Help us be good neighbors, Jesus of Nazareth.

A Remedy for Fear and Unhappiness

Anne Frank was a young Jewish girl who, along with her family, went into hiding in Amsterdam during the Nazi occupation of the Netherlands. Before they were captured and eventually died in a concentration camp, the Franks lived for two years in a few concealed rooms hidden behind a bookcase.

Frank's story became known to the world after her diary was found and published. Despite being confined to a small indoor space, the teenager never lost her love for nature and the outdoors, as this excerpt from her diary shows:

"The best remedy for those who are afraid, lonely or unhappy is to go outside, somewhere where they can be quite alone with the heavens, nature and God. Because only then does one feel that all is as it should be and that God wishes to see people happy, amidst the simple beauty of nature. As long as this exists, and it certainly always will, I know that then there will always be comfort for every sorrow, whatever the circumstances may be. And I firmly believe that nature brings solace in all troubles."

**Let heaven and earth praise Him.
(Psalm 69:34)**

Help me meditate on the beauty of Your creation, Father.

Little Faces of Mercy

Father Jeff Bayhi from the Diocese of Baton Rouge got the idea to create Metanoia Manor, a local home for sex trafficking victims. And he knew he wanted an order of nuns to run it. After doing some research, he found the Hospitaler Sisters of Mercy.

As reported by George Morris in the diocese's newspaper *The Advocate,* four Sisters were chosen to train at a similar facility in Italy to prepare for the new challenge. They will run Metanoia Manor, providing counseling, practical support and motherly love to its residents.

Father Bayhi believes the Sisters are the key to connecting with the victims. He said, "They have these nuns who look like little angels come in, and they care what happens to you. They just sit there and talk to you about you, and they're going to talk to you about being better, and you're not trash and God loves you and God wants something for you. Having the sisters there saying that, it completely changes the way the person sees themselves. I can't do that as a man...and cops can't do it. But these little faces of mercy can, and they're wonderful."

Give justice to the weak and the orphan. (Psalm 82:3)

Guide trafficking victims toward the help they need, Father.

700 Miles in Another's Shoes

When historian Anthony Cohen set out to retrace routes on the Underground Railroad, he recovered a piece of American history that few of us know.

Most of us are vaguely aware that the Underground Railroad was a series of trails and safe houses used by slaves on their exodus toward freedom. Yet, the perils and difficulties escape us. Anthony Cohen, an African-American, wanted to experience the same adversities and triumphs that those who traveled it knew.

He traced several routes and used several techniques to authenticate the slave's experience (he had himself shipped by box from Philly to New York as did Henry Brown in 1818). He walked, he hitched on wagons, he used the train. He spoke to schools and did research. He discovered unknown stops on the Railroad. Ultimately, he learned the bittersweet price of freedom.

Remember, God created us all for freedom. Let us use this great gift well.

My times are in Your hand; deliver me from... my enemies. (Psalm 31:15)

Help me, Lord, to respect the past in order to improve the future.

A Prayer for the Nation

Ours is a nation of many believers in God—or at least a Supreme Being. Yet how often do we ask our God to watch over us? This prayer will help us think about God and His people.

"God of liberty, we acknowledge Your reign. For the freedom of our land, for the rights we possess, for the security of our laws, we praise You and thank You.

"Give guidance to our leaders, watch over those who serve their country, raise up the poor, and exalt the humble. Make our nation great and strong, renowned in wisdom, prosperous in virtue, and renewed in faith.

"Destroy all signs of division: take away hatred and violence; fill us with Your peace. Make us one people, united in praising You. Amen."

The Lord said... "I will make of you a great nation, and I will bless you." (Genesis 12:1,2)

Father in Heaven and Creator of All, guide our country in establishing love, peace, justice, and mercy among all people.

Autistic Boy Gets Playdate to Remember

Living with autism and Tourette's syndrome, Austin Mendrala, age 11, had trouble finding other kids to play with. "Some kids are nice to him during the school year, but then he doesn't hear from them all summer," Austin's mother Delilah lamented to New Hampshire's *Union Leader Correspondent*. "My heart was just breaking for him."

Delilah took action by sending out a Facebook plea asking her son's friends, or anyone looking to make new friends, to meet them at their local school playground that Thursday. To the delight of both mother and son, two police cruisers showed up.

Merrimack police detective Chris Spillane was largely responsible for these officers' attendance after seeing Delilah's Facebook post and passing the message along to his department. Other young kids and even firefighters showed up as well. But Delilah was especially touched by the officers' kindness.

"The fact that they [police] took time out of their day to play with these kids and warm their hearts was impressive," Delilah concluded. "It was amazing."

Be kind to one another. (Ephesians 4:32)

Lord, may we be faithful and sincere in our friendships.

A Pioneering Aviator

Frank E. Petersen Jr., the first black aviator in the Marine Corps, had some interesting experiences along the way. He was arrested in an officers' club on suspicion of impersonating a lieutenant, and was told to repeat taking an exam because his superiors were convinced he cheated the first time around. While training in Florida, he was even ejected from a bus because he refused to move to the rear.

Still, Petersen endured. When he died in 2015 at the age of 83, he had the distinction of having been named the first black general in the Corps' long history. A trailblazer if ever there was one, he flew 350 combat missions during two tours—one in Korea, the other in Vietnam. Sam Roberts, who wrote his obituary in *The New York Times,* reported that he became the first of his race to command a fighter squadron, an air group, and a major air base.

All of his accomplishments gave him "a great satisfaction," he once said, but they also came with a challenge: "You thought you could perform before, but now you must perform again."

In every nation anyone who...does what is right is acceptable to Him. (Acts 10:34-35)

Remind us that we are all the same in Your eyes, Creator.

The Prayers of New Yorkers

Humans of New York is a popular online project created by Brandon Stanton in which he photographs and interviews random people on the streets of the city. In 2015, one person shared the following story:

"I got into a very desperate situation last year. I was under a lot of stress because my dad was in the hospital with a terminal illness. I didn't have much income, my credit was bad, and I needed a new place to live...I was completely despondent. So for the next two days, I walked around New York and asked hundreds of people to say a prayer for me. Or if they didn't want to pray, I asked them to say something nice to me.

"Most people just said: 'God bless you' or 'I hope things work out.' I asked priests, monks, bank tellers, security guards, homeless people, mentally ill people...everyone. I'd say that I approached about 200 people.

"Then, at the end of the two days, a post from a friend popped on my newsfeed. It said: 'I have an empty room and need someone to move in today.' So one of those prayers worked. I'm just not sure which one it was."

Ask, and it will be given you. (Matthew 7:7)

Christ, may I never undervalue the importance of human connections.

Foundation Helps Disabled Mom

Much of Danielle Hetland's life had been focused on serving those in need, specifically, by traveling the world with her husband on mission trips. But after one such trip to Southeast Asia in 2011, Hetland became the one who needed help.

The Hewitt, Texas resident contracted West Nile Virus, which caused brain swelling and permanent damage to some of the electrical systems that control body functions. For months, she couldn't care for herself or her family. And at times, she couldn't eat or talk.

While Hetland's condition improved, she still needed a motorized wheelchair to get around. Without money to afford one, she contacted the Advocates for Individuals with Disabilities Foundation at AID.org. They came through.

Hetland said, "My perspective has changed from shame and depression, to feeling proud for what I have overcome and look forward to where I am going. I now am looking to building a future (and getting out of the house more!) and contributing to life. Embracing changes is part of this process."

Every perfect gift is from above. (James 1:17)

Bring people with disabilities the help they need, Jesus.

An 'Irish Peasant's' Example

Peggy Noonan can be described in many ways: former speechwriter for President Reagan, *Wall Street Journal* columnist, and political commentator. But the "core of [her] identity," she says, is being Catholic.

During a "Christopher Closeup" interview about her collection of essays "The Time of Our Lives," Noonan credited her great-aunt Jane Jane with planting the seeds of her belief not through words, but through actions and symbols.

Noonan said, "[She] was a simple Irish peasant, and she had a simple Irish peasant's belief. She had on her bureau Mass cards and rosary beads and [pictures] of Jesus and the Sacred Heart and the Virgin Mary. And she was very kind.

"She took me to Mass when I was a little girl every Sunday, and I thought everybody in Mass was very nice, so I got it in my head that maybe if you go to church, you become nice. She didn't proselytize [or] teach me about Christ. She had Christ all around me."

Set the believers an example in speech and conduct, in love, in faith, in purity. (1 Timothy 4:12)

May my example plant seeds of faith in others' lives, Lord.

The Power of Symbols

Though best-selling author and former presidential speechwriter Peggy Noonan had the seeds of her Catholic faith planted by her aunt during childhood, her faith developed maturity and depth as she got older and learned more about Catholicism.

She even came to teach a religion class to girls at a private school in Manhattan for a number of years. They ranged in age from post-Communion to Confirmation, and they taught her a lesson about the influence (or lack thereof) of the pictures by which she had been surrounded growing up.

During an interview, Noonan said, "I asked [the girls], 'What signs and symbols of religious faith do you see around your house?' There was silence. Then one girl said, 'My grandmother wears a medal with Mary on it.' That was the only answer. I thought, 'Thank you, Grandma!' I enjoy seeing signs and symbols of faith in people's houses, whatever their faith is. I understand something's being said there. What's being said is, 'There is a God.' And it's important for kids to be aware of that."

**He is the image of the invisible God.
(Colossians 1:15)**

May my life point people towards You, Jesus.

On This Southern Ground...

The Zac Brown Band has won numerous Grammy Awards, along with other honors specific to the country music industry, such as CMA and ACM Awards. But the lead singer's dedication to children with special needs is worthy of accolades, too.

Brown is using proceeds from his concerts to build Camp Southern Ground in Peachtree City, Georgia, for children with autism and other special needs. He says: "As a former camp counselor, I know how a positive camp experience can transform a child's life. My dream is that children of all abilities will have an opportunity to experience the magic of the outdoors."

The camp's website notes their goal "is to provide extraordinary experiences for children to recognize and magnify the unique gifts within themselves and others in order to profoundly impact the world." They're already holding mini-camps that start off with the kids reciting the mantra, "On this Southern Ground, we will meet new friends, learn new things, and treat everyone with love and respect." Come to think of it, that's a pretty good mantra for all of us.

Extend hospitality to strangers. (Romans 12:13)

Enable me to bring out the best in others, Creator.

A New Detective's Tribute

In a promotion ceremony at One Police Plaza in New York City, Conor McDonald proudly wore his new detective's shield—which bore the same number as the officer who had helped save his father's life.

On July 12, 1986—while his wife was pregnant with Conor—NYPD Officer (later Detective) Steven McDonald was shot and paralyzed by a teenage bicycle thief. Now-retired Detective Brian Mulheren, whose badge number Conor McDonald selected, convinced Steven to get a critical hospital transfer at the time.

"My dad was on his deathbed," said Conor, a five-year veteran of the NYPD. "Brian pretty much knocked him to his senses and told him that he needed a second opinion."

John Annese, who covered the ceremony for the *Daily News,* reported that Mulheren said he was "honored" by Conor's thoughtful gesture. And Conor himself said, "I'm very emotional right now. It means a lot."

One generation shall laud Your works to another, and shall declare Your mighty acts. (Psalm 145:4)

God of our mothers and fathers, thank You for those who have gone before us and raised us up.

Cooking, Chemistry, and Community

Father Leo Patalinghug is a skilled cook who started the movement Grace Before Meals because he believes "the simple act of creating and sharing a meal can strengthen all kinds of relationships" and bring us closer to God. In 2014, he visited a San Diego school and met a young man named David Pack.

Pack recently wrote to Father Leo to share how this visit impacted him: "I started a project that combines my love of cooking, learning and my community and named it C3K. This stands for Cooking, Chemistry, and Community for Kids. I have been conducting some of my cooking classes at an orphanage in Tijuana. In my first class I made ice cream for them by showing them the science behind adding rock salt to crushed ice which causes the temperature to drop. The orphans loved it. I now go to Tijuana monthly to cook with them.

"I also have been cooking with homebound kids with chronic and terminal illnesses...I hope I have shown that food can bring joy to the ones who are making it as well as to the ones who are receiving it. Thank you for inspiring me!"

Whether you eat or drink...do everything for the glory of God. (1 Corinthians 10:31)

Help me to use food to build bonds of friendship, Lord.

Soledad O'Brien: Philanthropist

You probably know Soledad O'Brien through her television work. For many years, she anchored *CNN's* morning news program, and left in 2013 to start her own (very successful) production company. But did you know about Soledad O'Brien, philanthropist? She spoke about this facet of her life in an issue of the supplement *Spry Living* last year:

"My husband and I started the Starfish Foundation, which helps girls around the country go to—and get through—school. I saw young women getting scholarships for $2,500, and they were grateful, but they needed so much more—to pay for room, board, books...We also started the PowHERful Summit, a daylong conference full of practical information, like interview skills, personal finance and how to behave online."

O'Brien, 48, also learned about life along the way—and passed it on. "I've learned I can't help it if I'm not someone's cup of tea," she said. "The thing I can control is the quality of my work...I recognized that every single time I haven't been hired, something really cool came along instead."

Wisdom teaches her children, and gives help to those who seek her. (Sirach 4:11)

Jesus, Holy Wisdom, help me to grow wise and generous.

A Garden of Wisdom

An old Arabian proverb describes a book as "a garden carried in a pocket." That's a pretty image. And it's true.

Some books offer the serenity and beauty of a garden. They offer a retreat from our everyday cares. Others offer a garden's variety, showing experiences outside of our own lives.

But the most important thing a book shares is ideas. Ideas may be as vibrant as a landscape of bright flowers, or as subtle as the perfume of a single blossom. But when coupled with our reflections, they may lead us to wisdom.

That's a good reason to pick up a good book. Read it, think about it and share your thoughts and your books with others. Use your local library and encourage others to enjoy its possibilities.

[Make] your ear attentive to wisdom and [incline] your heart to understanding...cry out for insight, and raise your voice for understanding...then you will...find the knowledge of God. (Proverbs 2:1-5)

Enable me, Spirit of Wisdom, to seek You, to find You, and to embrace You.

Some Innovations Pay Off

If you ever look at a new item on the market and say, "Now, why didn't I think of that?" you have lots of company. Some things seem so obvious—after an inventor comes up with them.

Back in 1905, Frank Epperson accidentally froze a glass of lemonade with a stirrer in it. But, it wasn't until eighteen years later that he patented "frozen fruit water on a stick," also known as the Popsicle.

Epperson also came up with the Popsicle's famous "twin-stick." During the Great Depression he realized that customers had to feel like they were really getting their money's worth. With the second stick, two snack eaters could be happy for the price of one.

So if you have a flair for creativity or if you'd like to develop one, let your mind toy with different ideas. Exercise your capacity for discovery. You never know until you try.

Be rich in good works, generous, and ready to share. (1 Timothy 6:18)

Show me how to use the skills You've given me to make the world a better place, Creator.

A Powerful Force

"The desire to do something is a powerful force," singer-songwriter Emmylou Harris told a group of reporters over lunch recently. "I just believe the will is out there somewhere. It's all so overwhelming. But it's not impossible."

Harris, a multiple Grammy Award winner and living legend of American music, was not talking about the challenges of recording her next album. Instead, as she told *The Catholic Pulse's* Justin Catanoso, she was in Rome learning about the refugee crisis, in preparation for a concert tour to raise awareness of the needs of refugees and raise funds to help them. She is working with the Jesuit Refugee Services' Global Education Initiative, and she has hope that she can make a difference.

"I have faith in the goodness of people. Maybe because I've had such a blessed life," Harris told Catanoso. "I feel lucky in so many ways. And especially if you are a musician, an artist, and you make your living that way, in the best possible way, with so much joy, then you want to somehow give back."

What shall I return to the Lord for all His bounty to me? (Psalm 116:12)

Spirit of generosity, may I find opportunities to use the gifts You have given me in service to others.

Creating Change in the World

On his blog, entitled Grace Pending, Tom Zampino shared words from the late Trappist monk Thomas Merton about the way in which we should approach creating change in the world:

"Do not depend on the hope of results. You may have to face the fact that your work will be apparently worthless and even achieve no result at all, if not perhaps results opposite to what you expect...Start more and more to concentrate not on the results, but on the value, the rightness, the truth of the work itself. You gradually struggle less and less for an idea and more and more for specific people. In the end, it is the reality of personal relationship that saves everything."

Zampino also cited Pope Francis, who said: "To be open to a genuine encounter with others, 'a kind look' is essential. This is incompatible with a negative attitude that readily points out other people's shortcomings while overlooking one's own...Loving kindness builds bonds, cultivates relationships, creates new networks of integration and knits a firm social fabric."

How very good and pleasant it is when kindred live together in unity! (Psalm 133:1)

Help Your followers change the world through kindness, Lord.

A Rookie's Right Decision

By definition, Curtis Jackson is just a 44-year-old rookie from Brooklyn. But somehow, he knew just what to do when confronted by an attacker.

Jackson, a probationary sanitation worker, was with his partner when they stopped in at a convenience store in Manhattan one day last year. Suddenly, a man burst into the store, holding something that looked like a gun.

Being a former Marine and a big man who looks as if he'd have no trouble taking care of himself, Jackson quickly decided on a course of action. He charged down the aisle and pinned the assailant against a wall until police arrived. Pronouncing himself "not a political person," Jackson said he dislikes hearing anyone disparage what he's come to think of as "his city."

"New Yorkers look out for each other, for everybody," he told the *Daily News*. "We're team players. It's a big city, and we're here for each other."

Truly I tell you, just as you did it to one of the least of these who are members of My family, you did it to Me. (Matthew 25:40)

Lord Jesus, may I recognize and help You in those in need.

The No Boundaries Coalition

In 2015, the *Catholic Review* newspaper launched a series called "One Baltimore" to address racial and economic divisions in its hometown, highlight areas that needed support, and ideally, create more unity.

That's why the annual announcement of grants from the Catholic Campaign for Human Development (CCHD) were awaited with special interest. They would go to groups fighting poverty and systemic issues that lead to unrest. Would one of the organizations associated with "One Baltimore" win a grant? Yes.

The No Boundaries Coalition, based in St. Peter Claver Church, won $40,000 to promote healthy food options in Sandtown, a part of the city with a dearth of food choices. "Where I live, in Sandtown, we don't have a grocery store." said Melissa Kelly, a parishioner of St. Peter and chairwoman of the Coalition's health committee. "I can walk down the street and buy a bottle of vodka, but not an apple or a banana."

With CCHD's help, Sandtown's residents will get a nutrition boost—and the fruitful knowledge that somebody cares.

Do not be...tight-fisted toward your needy neighbor. (Deuteronomy 15:7)

Help me to create unity where there is division, Lord.

Turning Cancer Into Something Good

At age 12, Elana Simon was diagnosed with a rare liver cancer that required surgery. In 2016, at age 20, she spoke at a conference at the Vatican about a potential cure for the disease.

As reported by *CBS2-TV*, Simon thought she was done with cancer when she went into remission. But then she decided to investigate the problem by recording a Youtube video and "asking other young people with the same type of cancer to send in samples of their tumors, and 65 did. Under the supervision of her father, who is a scientist, she discovered a common mutation in each sample."

Though much of the Harvard University student's life has been devoted to researching cancer, she may not follow in her father's scientist footsteps. For now, though, she is happy to be part of such an important endeavor and was delighted to speak to the world's top cancer researchers at a conference held at the Vatican. She said, "It's good I was the person who ended up getting [this cancer] because it has turned into something good."

You have taken up my cause, O Lord, You have redeemed my life. (Lamentations 3:58)

Turn my pain into productivity, Divine Physician.

A Family Grows in the Pediatric Unit

Nicole was born in 2012 with a dire birth defect: her gastric organs were outside of her body. She spent several months in the University of New Mexico Hospital's Neonatal Intensive Care Unit before being transferred to the pediatric unit, where she still needed lots of help.

The nurse who cared for her there was Amber Boyd, 28, who became like family to the little girl since her biological parents had their rights taken away. Boyd got so attached to Nicole that she decided to make her a real member of the family.

She consulted with her husband Taylor, and they both agreed they could care for the child since her medical condition had improved. At first, the couple obtained a foster care license. Then, in 2016, they officially adopted her. It was an appropriate choice since Boyd herself had been adopted.

Now a happy adoptive Mom, Boyd told *ABC News,* "[Nicole] is spunky, she's sassy...She's always happy. She's seriously the strongest kid I've ever met."

God gives the desolate a home to live in. (Psalm 68:6)

There are children in this world who feel unwanted and unloved, Lord. Guide me in helping them if I can.

Food For Thought

Good nutrition is too important to be an afterthought. Parents, grandparents, teachers, and other wise adults know that youngsters need well-balanced meals to be at their best in school and ultimately in life. But the siren song of salty, fatty, fast food is loud, inexpensive, convenient, and often unhealthy.

Research shows how essential sound nutrition supports physical and mental well-being, according to a report in the *National Association of Social Workers* magazine.

For instance, children can't concentrate as well in school when they haven't had a good breakfast. Teenagers (often girls, but not always,) develop problems around food when they try to control things by binging and purging.

People on limited incomes might have to make tough choices between a healthy diet and necessary medications. Some elderly people face additional challenges when depression and loneliness curb their appetites. In other words, healthy food is vital. Let's not give it short shrift.

No one ever hates his own body, but he nourishes and tenderly cares for it. (Ephesians 5:29)

Lord, help us to nourish each other in body, mind and spirit.

Beauty After the Flood

Ann Cleland of Des Moines, Iowa, found her life turned upside down by the devastating floods that hit the Midwest in 1993. The waters broke right after she moved into a new home and renovated her beauty salon.

Her home and business were ruined. Her teenage daughter dealt with serious grief and depression. Cleland spent days working at a local beauty parlor and nights rebuilding her salon. She felt lonely and helpless, but she found kindness in friends and strangers alike.

Volunteers from her church helped her clean her house. People in Connecticut sent her $500. A man redesigned her salon at little cost and volunteers fixed her plumbing and wiring for free. Cleland was amazed at how helpful people were to each other. She said, "Month after month of God's compassionate provision changed my fear to renewed faith."

Stretch out Your hand from on high; set me free and rescue me from the mighty waters. (Psalm 144:7)

Lord, rescue me from "mighty waters," and remind me to offer others a helping hand when they feel like they're drowning.

Have You Heard?

Even scrupulously honest people can unwittingly spread false information. At some time or another, most of us have repeated a rumor that proved to be untrue. And even true stories easily become so distorted that they have little relation to fact.

Psychologists have identified common ways stories change as they pass from person to person: incidents may be exaggerated to make a more dramatic story; details may be forgotten, or what people hear may be influenced by their prejudices.

Rumors can damage businesses, ruin reputations, ignite racial and religious tensions—at the very least needless anxiety.

When you hear a story, ask yourself, "What's the source of this story?" and, "Is there any real evidence to support it?" Don't unthinkingly pass on rumors that could do harm. Take responsibility for your words.

Rumor follows rumor. (Ezekiel 7:26)

Lord, make my speech charitable, honest, wise, and joy-filled.

'The Greatest Kind of Hero'

For months there had been speculation about the name of the new Staten Island ferry. Would it honor a well-known American? Would it honor a native New Yorker, perhaps someone from the borough itself?

When the name was finally announced last year, just about everyone was pleased. The new ferry, which goes into service two years from now, will be named for Staff Sgt. Michael Ollis, 24, an Army veteran who died a hero's death in Afghanistan. In 2013, Ollis saved another soldier's life by throwing himself on a grenade tossed by a suicide bomber.

"Sgt. Ollis proved himself the greatest kind of hero," proclaimed New York Mayor Bill de Blasio. "He was so devoted to his country he was willing to put his life on the line more than once. Whatever he did, wherever he went, others were inspired by his leadership."

Erin Durkin, who covered the announcement for the *Daily News,* noted that the selection was endorsed by 5,000 New Yorkers who signed a petition to that effect.

No one has greater love than this, to lay down one's life for one's friends. (John 15:13)

Divine Master, may we honor the heroes of our nation.

Thrive in Joy, Part One

Easter is the celebration of Christ's resurrection—the event that makes our redemption possible, allowing us to reunite with our family and friends some day in heaven. That's a comforting thought for anyone who's lost a loved one, such as Jay and Mary Fagnano. On July 27, 2014, their 20-year-old son Nick was killed by a lightning strike at a California beach.

Nick had always embraced his relationship with Christ and put his faith into action. But Jay and Mary didn't know how deep that faith went until they found an essay he had written about heaven for a college English class. It read:

"Regardless of heaven being beyond my comprehension, the afterlife that I want to be a part of involves joy, excitement, and gratitude, as we will finally be reunited with the loved ones that we have lost on earth. Perhaps 'rest in peace' is actually not the best term in relation to death; rather, a phrase such as 'thrive in joy' best represents how I will want to spend eternity."

Jay and Mary looked at each other with tears streaming down their faces and said, "Nick is talking to us."

Everyone who believes in Him...may have eternal life. (John 3:16)

Guide me toward a joy-filled eternity with You, Jesus.

Thrive in Joy, Part Two

Reading their deceased son Nick's essay about heaven not only brought spiritual and emotional comfort to Jay and Mary Fagnano, it also inspired them to keep their son's name alive in a way that reflected the type of person he was. They founded the Thrive in Joy Nick Fagnano Foundation.

Nick had always been devoted to helping others through his church. And as a 13-year-old, he took it upon himself to collect baseball equipment for kids in the Dominican Republic who couldn't afford their own balls, gloves, and bats. Therefore, one of their outreach efforts takes place in the Dominican Republic at Tia Tatiana, a Christian school in the worst slum in Santo Domingo. Thrive in Joy has given them a new computer lab and provided necessary renovations.

Regarding their mission, Jay said, "If [Mary and I] can bring some joy to vulnerable children here and abroad, then I am giving glory to God. I am doing God's work. And it's Nick that's guiding us each and every day."

May the Lord of heaven...guide and prosper you both this night and grant you mercy and peace. (Tobit 7:11)

Guide me in bringing joy to the less fortunate, Father.

Rescued On the Side of the Road

Many years ago, 12 youths from Long Island, New York, came up with a unique service to motorists. For nearly a year, they happily surprised large numbers of drivers in distress on the highways.

Whenever they saw anyone stopped because of a flat tire, no gasoline, or minor engine trouble, they drove up, took care of the problem, and then went on their way without accepting any pay for their service.

The boys, between 17 to 21 years old, said that they formed their group, "The Courtesy Club," because they wanted "to do something useful that would keep them out of trouble."

If millions of young people would show similar initiative and enterprise in thinking up ways of their own to serve others, the possibilities for good would be innumerable. Encourage young people to be resourceful in discovering and putting to use the talent that God has entrusted to every one of them.

He raises up the needy out of distress, and makes their families like flocks. (Psalm 107:41)

Inspire young people, O Lord, to show originality in devising ways to serve others.

Getting Your Priorities Straight

In his nearly 40 years as a news anchor and reporter in New York City, Ernie Anastos has earned more than 30 Emmy Awards and nominations, the Edward R. Murrow Award, and a place in the New York State Broadcasters Hall of Fame.

To what does he attribute his longevity? He once told interviewer Bob Nesoff, "I look at issues and problems that I report on with a sense of finding solutions and a belief that we can make things better. It's called 'hope.'"

We were happy to honor Anastos with our 2016 Christopher Life Achievement Award for his professional and charitable accomplishments—and because of the person he is. This devoted husband and father has his priorities straight—and they're priorities from which we can all learn.

As he told interviewer Markos Papadatos, "I feel successful because I have a family that I love and people who respect my work, and a sense of purpose in my life. Most important is my faith in God. After that, everything else falls into place."

In all your ways acknowledge Him, and He will make straight your paths. (Proverbs 3:6)

Remind me to put my life's priorities straight, Savior.

Look for the Good Points

"Fly swatters" is the name one editor gives to those individuals who read papers and magazines only to spot small errors and write abusive letters about them. Such people highlight mistakes while ignoring good points.

Scolding, abusing, or humiliating the one to whom you are writing can defeat your very objectives. Reasonable criticism, on the other hand, can achieve much good if it offers specific, constructive suggestions on how to make improvements.

One friendly, positive recommendation can often accomplish more than a bucketful of complaints. Then, too, a blend of Christian courtesy with firmness is apt to win the other person's consideration rather than his indifference or hostility.

Stick to the divine formula which enables you to disagree without being disagreeable. In short, write letters to others using the same tone you wish them to employ when writing to you, and you will be heading in the right direction.

Do not find fault before you investigate; examine first, and then criticize. (Sirach 11:7)

O Lord, help me to be mindful of what is right with the world and not exaggerate what is wrong.

What God Has Called You to Do

Actress Patricia Heaton is known for her comedic roles on "Everybody Loves Raymond" and "The Middle." But in 2006, she took on a producing role for the Christopher Award-winning film "Amazing Grace." It told the story of William Wilberforce, who helped end the slave trade in England during the 1800s.

Both faith and action are central to the movie. During a "Christopher Closeup" interview, Heaton said, "Wilberforce's faith is what propelled him to take on this huge commitment—and the fact that he was able to apply his faith to a social problem was very important. Probably the only thing that was able to keep him going was his faith because it literally took 40 years...

"Wilberforce was shunned from society. He used to be a bon vivant, and then was disinvited to be with the 'cool' people and had to hang out with all the Christian abolitionists...There's a price to pay, and I think that is one of the messages: you have to be willing to sacrifice everything to follow God and what He's called you to do."

If any want to become My followers, let them...take up their cross and follow Me. (Matthew 16:24)

Give me the strength to follow You in the face of opposition, Father.

Usher's Words of Marital Wisdom

The late Frank Potenza used to be an usher at St. Patrick's Cathedral in New York City, greeting hundreds of visitors each day with warm smiles and personal hellos. The friendliness and concern he showed people prompted many locals to make a stop at the Cathedral part of their daily routine.

One day, a young couple came seeking his advice and encouragement. They were a bit discouraged by the concerns they faced in preparing for marriage.

"I'm going to share a secret with you," explained Potenza. "Problems will always be there. It's how you deal with them that's important, so concentrate on two simple things as a couple. Patience and faith. Above all else, develop these two things and be sure to develop them as a couple. When you have these, you wake up in the morning and things just seem easier."

May you be made strong with all the strength that comes from His glorious power, and may you be prepared to endure everything with patience. (Colossians 1:11)

Lord, help me embrace the virtues of patience and faith.

A Dog's Spiritual Lessons, Part One

Jeffrey Bruno, the art director for the website Aleteia, has had a lifelong connection with and love for dogs. He remembers one in particular, a German shepherd named Beatrice, who suffered from a degenerative disease which left her unable to walk. Caring for Beatrice taught Bruno many lessons not just about dogs, but about life, love, and God. Here are a few:

- "The pure sense of joy that dogs have...seems to be connected to how much they are willing to hope, and to be vulnerable, and to be satisfied with small things. It suggests to me that if we want to know a similar joy, we need to open ourselves up to the Holy Spirit, be willing to hope and see the value in the small gifts that God bestows on us, every day."

- "Even when you're wrapped up in the troubles of life and the world, a dog is completely attentive and undistracted; you are their world. There is a good lesson in there, about giving attention to our family members, but a bigger lesson is this: when we turn to God, He isn't distracted by the troubles of the world either; we are the world to Him."

Your steadfast love is better than life. (Psalm 63:3)

Father, I thank You for the gift of Your love and attention.

A Dog's Spiritual Lessons, Part Two

Today, more of Jeffrey Bruno's lessons about life, love, and God as learned from his dog Beatrice:

- "Over the years my wife and I raised two wonderful children and cared for some elder members of our family, but it was Beatrice, who needed her diapers changed and to be carried from room to room after she lost the use of her legs, who taught us about graciously, humbly accepting our care. The lesson? There is no shame in needing help from people who love us; it gives them a chance to express that love in a different way that might actually be fuller and more honest. In the long run, our humility in accepting help from others may assist in their salvation too."

- "Feeling a dog lay up against you is a wonderful thing, and it banishes loneliness. Often we forget that. We get wrapped up in our personal woe, and feel isolated, and then suddenly, the dog is there. You're not alone. God is always there too, and yes, we can forget that. We may have a dog's companionship for a few years, but we have God's companionship for all eternity."

The free gift of God is eternal life in Christ Jesus our Lord. (Romans 6:23)

May I be humble as I strive for eternal life with You, Jesus.

'You Never Know When It Could Be You'

When disaster strikes, Catholic Charities of Southeast Texas is ready to move right in—and when disaster response coordinator Tara Byars describes it as a "rewarding job," she knows whereof she speaks. "You never know when it could be you," she added. "I can vouch for that because in October of 2015, my house flooded. It helped me to understand and share a closer experience with the people I serve."

The program she coordinates helps people by providing emergency assistance of all types, according to a story in the *East Texas Catholic* by Mallory Matt. Byars is proud of what they do, too: "We help people who are homeless or about to become homeless, single moms, and domestic violence and drug trafficking victims. We see it all here."

Catholic Charities makes sure that none are forgotten. Its programs even include Elijah's Place, which gives peer and adult support to children, ages five to 18, who are grieving the loss of a parent or a sibling.

Religion that is pure and undefiled before God, the Father, is this: to care for orphans and widows in their distress. (James 1:27)

Father, may I always be present for those grieving a loss.

'I Want You to Be Yourself'

Vin Scully was remembering New York City in the old days, and told Dan Pietrafasa of *Catholic New York* about some words of advice he'd gotten from Red Barber, the legendary Brooklyn Dodgers' broadcaster.

Scully is a legend himself as the on-air man for the Los Angeles Dodgers and in line for retirement this year at the age of 88. He said Barber told him, "I want you to be yourself because there is no one else like you." Spoken like a true Christopher!

Scully, a Fordham University graduate who grew up in the shadow of the George Washington Bridge, remembers New York from the '30s and '40s: "It was marvelous...We had simple, hardworking people. We had a lot of things you need in a neighborhood like a department store, grocery store and meat market."

Scully concluded, "We were in our own little world...New York is a part of my life even though I'm not there anymore."

All must test their own work; then that work, rather than their neighbor's work, will become a cause for pride. (Galatians 6:4)

Father, help me to be the unique person You created me to be.

Dr. Heimlich's Heimlich

By now the story has become something of a cliché: a diner who is out for the evening suddenly finds that he or she is choking, when a stranger steps in and applies the Heimlich maneuver. The diner's life is saved and everyone goes on his way.

It happened mostly that way last year in Cincinnati to Patty Ris, 87. The one exception: the "stranger" was none other than Dr. Henry J. Heimlich, 96, the originator of the maneuver that bears his name. He was eating dinner at the Deupree House retirement home when he saw Ris choking.

"I made a fist," he said, "with my right hand—you can do it with either hand, by the way—and put my arms around her. I did it three times, and it apparently was pretty much done on the first time. A piece of meat with a little bone attached flew out of her mouth."

Dr. Heimlich developed the move in 1974, but this was the first time he's been called on to administer the maneuver himself. At 96, he showed he still knows just what to do.

The living, they thank You, as I do today. (Isaiah 38:19)

Lord, may I never be too young or too old to save a life!

From the Anchor Desk to the Pulpit

Before entering a Catholic seminary, Nick Adam was a local television news anchor—covering everything, he told *Extension* magazine, "from tornado touchdowns to local elections and sporting events."

But what he really wanted was to study for the priesthood, and he explained why: "I am inspired by the people of my parish in Meridian, Mississippi, and by the example of my pastor there. The Lord has put this call on my heart and has asked me to discern what life as a priest would be like.

"Throughout my seminary journey, this call has grown stronger and I am more excited than ever to start ministering with the people of the Diocese of Jackson."

Adam received support from Catholic Extension for his summer program, and he's grateful for it. "I experienced the love of God," he said. "I realized that my first objective must be to cultivate my relationship with the Lord in prayer, and out of that prayer come fruits in ministry."

But [Jesus] would withdraw to deserted places and pray. (Luke 5:16)

Lord, may I always make time to be with You in prayer.

A Company with a Heart

When Laura Fanucci was pregnant with her twin daughters Maggie and Abby, she bought maternity clothes from the online clothing and fashion service Stitch Fix. Tragically, both girls died shortly after childbirth due to a blood disorder.

Fanucci kept receiving emails from Stitch Fix's maternity department, however, so she contacted them to explain what happened and asked that they remove her from their maternity list. She also asked them to send her some regular clothes in purple because that color reminded her of Maggie and Abby.

That package arrived and, some time later, a new box did as well, even though Fanucci had not ordered anything. It was a beautiful sympathy note along with the gift of a silver bracelet with the initials of her late daughters as well as her three sons.

Fanucci was floored by the company's kindness. She shared the story on Facebook, and concluded by saying, "Let's BE these exceptional humans today: the ones that notice need, dig deeper, take time, and reach out. The ones who give more than anyone expects. The ones who do their work with love—and turn other people's days upside down with joy."

Let us work for the good of all. (Galatians 6:10)

Where there is sadness, let me bring joy, Lord.

The Belief of The 33

"I choose to believe we'll all get out." So says Mario Sepulveda (Antonio Banderas) to his fellow miners in the movie "The 33," which was inspired by the true story of the 33 Chileans who became trapped 2,300 feet underground when the mine in which they were working collapsed in 2010.

The film takes viewers not only into the miners' experiences, but also the uphill battle their families fought to get the mining company and government to make rescue efforts.

The miners know they're working a dangerous job, so faith is a part of their lives. They make the sign of the cross as they enter the mine and turn to prayer for strength after the collapse. And when an alcoholic miner going through withdrawal admits he doesn't know how to pray for help, a friend tells him that God doesn't care what words he uses—then the two pray together.

"The 33" reminds viewers to call on God during times of trouble (and hopefully in good times as well), while also demonstrating that human ingenuity can solve seemingly impossible problems.

The people who walked in darkness have seen a great light. (Isaiah 9:2)

Even when I can't see You, Lord, help me believe.

I Still Got It!

It's never too late to pursue new dreams—or old dreams, as the case may be. Just ask Donny Most. You'll remember him as playing funny man Ralph Malph on the 1970s sitcom "Happy Days." He was the guy with the catch phrase, "I still got it!"

In addition to acting, Most has always been passionate about music. At age 14, he was already singing at resorts in New York's Catskill Mountains. But when "Happy Days" came along, he gave it up. Though he could have started again when the series ended, the type of music he loves wasn't popular then.

Most told the *Palm Beach Post,* "What I love is the Great American Songbook with a jazz bent—Sinatra, some Count Basie and Bobby Darin—but it was hard to do that in the 1970s and 1980s when it was still looked upon as your parents' or grandparents' music. But Harry Connick Jr. broke through, then Tony Bennett did the *MTV* thing...Eventually I thought, 'If I'm gonna do this, I'd better start now.' My first gig was July 2014, and the reaction has been incredible. People are blown away. They say, 'You're the real deal. Why'd you wait so long?'"

Your work shall be rewarded. (2 Chronicles 15:7)

Guide me in the pursuit of new goals, Holy Spirit.

Be a Friend to Those Who Grieve

Kirsten Andersen recalled a childhood friend who was killed in an accident, leaving behind a wife and two young sons. In the days following his funeral, this grieving family was surrounded by mourners and people supporting them. But Andersen realized that as the days and months pass, that family's grief may be less evident, but still present—and that holds true for anyone who loses a loved one.

Writing on the website Aleteia, she suggests, "Send a card, flowers, gift or note to someone on the six-month anniversary of his or her loved one's death...Better yet, invite the person out to lunch or dinner and ask how she's doing, face to face. Let her know you remember what she's lost. If she's feeling up to it, chat about all the great memories. I guarantee she'll appreciate it."

Andersen concludes by advising readers to use technology to set yearly or twice-yearly reminders: "Keep the promise you made when the grief was fresh: don't forget the lost."

Religion that is pure and undefiled...is this: to care for orphans and widows in their distress, and to keep oneself unstained by the world. (James 1:27)

Remind me to comfort the grieving and lonely, Creator.

Lifeline in a War Zone

"I'm too scared to leave," says Fatimatou Zalingo, one of the thousands of innocent Muslims who fled her home in Central Africa because of violent clashes between two militia groups fighting for power. Now settled with her family in an enclave in the village of Boda, she shares a small home with two other families, but still fears an attack if she crosses a road that divides Boda.

Catholic Relief Services is doing what it can to ease life for these refugees. Michael Stulman, the CRS regional information director based in Dakar, Senegal, wrote about Zalingo in *The Wooden Bell,* the organization's publication. He explained that CRS, working with support from its partners, is aiding more than 13,000 displaced families with emergency firewood and other living supplies—and Zalingo is one of them.

Together, they're helping those with nowhere else to turn become self-reliant. In the process, they sow seeds of hope in a land wracked with fear and despair.

**We are afflicted in every way, but not crushed; perplexed, but not driven to despair.
(2 Corinthians 4:8)**

Bring peace to those enduring war and violence, Father.

In Times of Trouble

Leslie Guenther has learned where to turn when she's in trouble—and she was in big trouble a few years ago. She was seven months pregnant and had to be rushed to the hospital for emergency surgery to deliver her child prematurely. But her husband was deployed in Afghanistan, her two sons were fast asleep, and her closest family members were five states away.

Thankfully, her mother-in-law knew just what to do. She contacted the Red Cross, which through its Emergency Communications Center—available seven days a week, 24 hours a day—arranged a flight home for Leslie's husband to rush to the hospital.

Leslie later told *CrossNotes*, a publication of the American Red Cross North Jersey Region, that the surgery was a difficult one and surgeons had to put her in a medically-induced coma. "I woke up three days later to my husband's hands holding my hand," Leslie said, "telling me that our daughter was alive, and we were going to make it."

He will command His angels concerning you to guard you in all your ways; on their hands they will bear you up. (Psalm 91:11-12)

Loving Father, I trust that Your angels will protect me.

Screen Legend's Nightly 'Hail Mary'

Acting legend Maureen O'Hara died at age 95 in 2015, but she left a legacy of great films including "Miracle on 34th Street" and "The Quiet Man."

O'Hara was also never shy about citing the importance of her Catholic faith. Her belief in God never wavered, even through personal tragedies like the death of her husband and her own bout with cancer.

In his book "Maureen O'Hara: The Biography," author Aubrey Malone revealed more about the actress's religious devotion: "When O'Hara was in her late eighties, a journalist asked her the secret of her longevity. She replied, 'Say your Hail Mary every night when you go to bed.'

"Such a devotion seems to sum her up. No matter who she kissed or killed onscreen, no matter how many convolutions attended her lengthy life, she hung on to the simple 'Ave Maria' for direction. She often made statements that affirmed her faith. 'How could you have had such a wonderful life as me,' she asked, 'if there wasn't a God directing?'"

Lead me in Your truth, and teach me, for You are the God of my salvation. (Psalm 25:5)

Creator, direct my life and help me to trust in You.

Bread and Life

Sister Bernadette Szymczak began a soup kitchen in the Bedford-Stuyvesant section of Brooklyn in 1982. Partly because of government cutbacks, the need to feed the hungry was becoming urgent.

At her death 16 years later, the Bread and Life Soup Kitchen served a thousand hot meals every weekday and was the biggest such facility in New York City.

But Sister Bernadette did more than fill empty stomachs. She helped people change their lives through a program with medical, job replacement, adult education and other projects.

Bill Baker, a drug addict fresh out of jail, stopped by for coffee. Sister Bernadette asked him to help carry some trays. Over the years, he became a full-time volunteer and, finally, a member of the staff. Says Baker, "She turned my life around. She never gave up on me."

Perhaps that is Sister Bernadette Szymczak's greatest legacy—never giving up. May the same be said of us.

Feed My lambs...Feed My sheep. (John 21:15,17)

There are so many ways to serve. Help me find my way to give, Lord and Brother of us all.

The Love of Friends

"A friend is one to whom one may pour out all the contents of one's heart, chaff and grain together, knowing that the gentlest of hands will take and sift it, keep what is worth keeping and, with a breath of kindness, blow the rest away."

Those thoughtful words of an Arabian proverb are true. A real friend sees us for what we are and loves us both because of it and in spite of it. We help each other, comfort each other and tell the truth to each other.

"The Book of Common Prayer" offers this lovely petition: "Almighty God, we entrust all who are dear to us to Thy never-failing care and love, for this life and the life to come; knowing that Thou art doing for them better things than we can desire or pray for."

Wine and music gladden the heart, but the love of friends is better than either. (Sirach 40:20)

Thank You for the friends who love me and whom I love, Lord. Allow me to bring Your blessing to them when next we meet.

Rooftop Rescue

Robert Martie could hardly believe his eyes. There was his 77-year-old neighbor, hanging upside down by his foot from a second-floor deck rail of his home. Martie didn't have time to ask how he got there; he only had time to act, freeing the man's foot and saving him from serious injury or death. The borough council in Kinnelon, New Jersey, gave him its heroism award, and police pieced together this sequence of events:

The older man had been enjoying the sunshine on his deck with his daughter when he got up to get something inside. Suddenly he felt light-headed and lost his balance, stumbling backwards and falling over the deck rail. His foot became wedged, and there he was—two stories off the ground.

Alerted by the young woman's screams, Martie, who was home that morning doing yard work, rushed to rescue him, freed his foot and brought him down to safety. Deborah Walsh wrote up the story in the pages of *Suburban Trends*, noting that Martie attended the council meeting as a tribute to all emergency responders.

Which of these three was a neighbor? (Luke 10:36)

Jesus, help me listen for and answer the cry of my neighbor in distress.

Infusing Christ into Education

Almost from the start, the Catholic Extension Society has been funding Catholic campus efforts. First came the construction of churches in predominantly rural areas, and then came seminary education. Then bishops began to write in, asking if Extension couldn't help fund campus ministry programs. So it did, and now promises to even further expand its efforts.

That's the word from Bishop Edward J. Slattery, the long-time president of Extension, who retired last year as Bishop of Tulsa, Oklahoma. "The great thing about campus ministry," he said in the summer issue of *Extension* magazine, "is that the efforts of evangelization on college campuses have lasting effects on those who participate. Young people who are exposed to many secular efforts in college have that balanced by infusing Christ and His Church into their education."

Bishop Slattery said it's important for young adults to get to know one another in the context of the Church—"so they realize that there are others like them who are struggling to find the truth of Jesus and the Gospel."

Make disciples of all nations. (Matthew 28:19)

Fill young people with the truth of Your word, Father.

Watch Out for the Pimples of Sin!

We all know that letting the sun go down on our anger is a bad idea. Spiritually speaking, it can be downright ugly.

In a recent reflection at Aleteia, writer Joanne McPortland compares going to bed without making up to going to bed without removing the day's makeup. Both let dirt and grunge build up, blocking the pores of the skin or the soul. Both can lead to inflammation, the fiery infection that shows itself in outbreaks of blemishes and the pimples of sin.

Like a nightly skin care regimen, cleansing ourselves of anger and irritation at the end of each day works best when we make a ritual of it. Consciously asking forgiveness of and granting forgiveness to family members can be as simple as adding a line to evening prayers.

Those of us who live alone can reach out with a quick phone call or text to those with whom we interact. It's important to make up with ourselves, too—and of course, with God.

Do not let the sun go down on your anger. (Ephesians 4:27)

Forgiving Father, prompt me to make peace with myself, with others, and with You before the sun goes down.

The Pope in the Congregation

What do you do if you're a priest on your way to celebrate Mass and you're told that none other than Pope Francis himself is sitting in the front pew? You swallow twice and go on with your plans. That's what Msgr. Lucio Bonora did.

It happened a couple of years ago in St. Peter's Basilica, at 7 a.m. Aug. 21—the feast of St. Pius X. Pope Francis prayed for his predecessor at the sainted pope's tomb, where a previously-scheduled Mass was about to begin. The celebrant was to be Msgr. Bonora, an official at the Vatican Secretariat of State. When a basilica employee told him of his distinguished congregation—the pope and about 70 others—Msgr. Bonora hesitated for a moment, then began. He's glad he did!

At the sign of peace, he stepped down and greeted the Holy Father, who then stood in line to receive Communion. After Mass, Pope Francis told Msgr. Bonora that he went to the tomb to pray for all catechists on the saint's feast day—"as I did every year in Argentina." It was a memorable encounter the Monsignor will never forget.

The prayers of both of them were heard. (Tobit 3:16)

Teach us to pray humbly and sincerely together, Creator.

Support Your Local Deli

Here's a deli man who really knows his onions—and his customers. Yogendra "Yogi" Patel, and his wife, Vilsa, operate the Leprechaun News, a deli in Rutherford, New Jersey, where they sell, among many items, tickets for the New Jersey Lottery. One day, Yogi discovered that a million-dollar scratch-off ticket had registered in the store's computer. Apparently the winning ticket had been sold in the deli, but no one had come forward to claim the prize. The unusually large amount set the owner to thinking—who could have bought the winning ticket?

Yogi thought back to his regular customers, and remembered that one of them was a lottery devotee. Sure enough, his gamble paid off. The patron had bought the ticket, but mistakenly discarded it. Yogi was able to reunite him with the winning slip. A local politician honored Yogi for his honesty, but the deli owner kept his priorities in perspective all the while.

"I was happy to be honored by the assemblyman," he said. "But I was happier when I was able to give the ticket back."

We intend to do what is right not only in the Lord's sight but also in the sight of others. (2 Corinthians 8:21)

May I always choose honesty and integrity, Divine Judge.

A Giant Comes Through for Kids

Victor Cruz, the New York Giants outstanding wide receiver, has never forgotten that he comes from Paterson, New Jersey. Neither has the city's former mayor, now U.S. Rep. Bill Pascrell, who paid tribute to Cruz's love for his hometown while introducing him at a gathering in Paterson last year.

Ed Rumley covered the presentation for *The Record* of Hackensack. The event honored Cruz at a fundraiser for the national park at the Great Falls of the Passaic River, the spot where Alexander Hamilton envisioned his plans to make Paterson the nation's first industrial city. "Victor has cared about kids from Paterson in a very tangible way," Pascrell said.

The Hamilton Partnership presented Cruz with an award for his extensive work with the city. The Giants' star helps sponsor a summer technology program, an event he said followed a similar program he had seen at the White House. "I wanted the same thing for kids from Paterson," he explained.

The advantage of knowledge is that wisdom gives life to the one who possesses it. (Ecclesiastes 7:12)

Instill young people with a thirst for knowledge, Lord, and inspire adults to teach them well.

'Get Up, Shave, and Choose Life'

In a house fire started by a hot plate, Brooklyn, New York father Gabriel Sassoon lost seven of his children. His wife Gayle was seriously injured and had to be placed in a medically-induced coma. Their 15-year-old daughter was hurt in the fire, but survived.

Initially, Gayle thought the children had escaped the flames by jumping out of a window. When she learned the truth, she mourned, but ultimately chose to lean on her faith, saying in Hebrew, "Blessed is the true judge."

Meanwhile, Gabriel felt so devastated that he considered suicide. Thankfully, he abandoned these thoughts and grew determined to help others deal with life's challenges instead.

As reported by New York's *Daily News*, it took a while for Gabriel to transition from being a private family man to "a public person." But he said, "I felt that I needed to decide whether I wanted to live or not. I told myself, 'Get up, clip your nails, shave and choose life. You still have work to do in this world.'"

If the earthly tent we live in is destroyed, we have a building from God...eternal in the heavens. (2 Corinthians 5:1)

Comfort those who mourn the loss of their children, Lord.

How a Priest Overcame Stuttering

By his own admission, Caridade Drago "stuttered terribly" as a youth in India. He hated both the children who made fun of him and the grownups who pitied him. But as time went on, the decision that he wanted to become a priest grew stronger in his mind—and he realized that he was in for a rough journey. Sure enough, a seminary rector turned him down because of his stammer, with the explanation, "Priests preach and teach."

Still, Drago persisted and improved somewhat in his speaking, joining a Jesuit novitiate and hoping that he'd be ordained someday. Thanks to a compassionate spiritual guide, he continued to improve, and after many years as a Jesuit-in-training, he received his letter of approval for ordination. The glorious day came and went, and Father Drago reflected on his situation for *America*, the Jesuit weekly.

"Do I stammer today?" he asked. "Yes, sometimes. But when I feel the stutter coming, I attend to the presence of God and His unconventional love. Immediately my fears vanish and peace fills my heart. I face others calmly, and talk without fear."

You shall speak whatever I command you. Do not be afraid...for I am with you. (Jeremiah 1:7-8)

Father, be with me as I use my gifts in Your service.

Your Ideas are Needed

Too few of us know how to express ourselves adequately and, because of this, we fail to spread the good ideas entrusted to us by God. Because of such neglect, the positions of influence often go by default into the hands of those who are determined to mislead rather than lead.

Take advantage of every opportunity to communicate good ideas. These few tips may help:

- **Remember your importance as a connecting link between God and others.** You may be the transmitter of divine truth to many a person who would never hear it except for you.
- **Acquaint yourself with some fundamentals of public speaking and effective writing.**
- **Above all else, deepen your convictions—your love of God and people.** You will never stimulate others to action if words come only from your lips, not from your heart.

If I speak in the tongues of mortals and of angels, but do not have love, I am a noisy gong or a clanging cymbal. (1 Corinthians 13:1)

Thanks to You, Holy Spirit, for the privilege of being a preacher of Your divine truth.

'God Was Right in My Face'

Joy can be found through "faithful suffering," through trusting that God can bring good even out of tragedy. That's an idea that "Heaven is for Real" writer-director Randall Wallace was left with after a girl named D'Asia reacted to his movie.

"Heaven is For Real" told the story of Colton Burpo, a three-year-old boy in Nebraska who claims he visited heaven when he almost died during emergency surgery. D'Asia said the movie affirmed her faith because it left her feeling "that God was right in my face."

During a "Christopher Closeup" interview, Wallace said, "When she was nine or ten years old, she was in a car accident that paralyzed her from the neck down. Her attitude is that her accident was a great gift because she got to know the loving doctors and nurses who care for her. So [the idea] that joy is a byproduct of faithful suffering is certainly accurate in her case."

After you have suffered for a little while, the God of all grace...will Himself restore, support, strengthen, and establish you. (1 Peter 5:10)

When pain and disappointment darken my spirits, Lord, guide me back into Your light.

A Little Less Messy

In her syndicated column, Kathryn Jean Lopez cited a story that Washington, D.C.'s Cardinal Donald Wuerl shared about an encounter he had at Harvard University while being part of a panel discussion with other religious leaders about faith in a pluralistic society. A law professor and self-proclaimed atheist asked, "What do you people think you bring to our society?"

Cardinal Wuerl answered, "What do you think the world would be like if it were not for the voices of all of those religious traditions represented in the hall?...What would our culture be like had we not heard religious imperatives such as, 'Love your neighbor as yourself, Do unto others as you would have them do unto you'? How much more harsh would our land be if we did not grow up hearing...'Blessed are the merciful, blessed are the peacemakers'? What would the world be like had we never been reminded that we will have to answer to God for our actions?"

"The atheist got the point," wrote Lopez, "and acknowledged that without the leavening influence of people living their faith, the world 'would be a mess!'"

Conduct yourselves honorably. (1 Peter 2:12)

Help me to create a better, more loving world, Creator.

Magdalena House

For 17 years, the mission of French priest Father Jean-Philippe Chauveau has been rescuing young women in the vicinity of Paris from lives of prostitution. In 2016, he achieved a new milestone. The bishop of Meaux is allowing him to use an old monastery to create Magdalena House, a facility where these girls can live together while pursuing a different life.

Father Chauveau told the website Aleteia that the girls frequently come from "chaotic lives often marked by domestic violence and all forms of abuse." As such, they are lonely because they've never made any genuine friendships.

The staff of Magdalena House hopes to rectify that by focusing on prayer and fellowship as well as practical skills. "Some of the girls have told me they would like to learn to knit," said the priest. "All of them want to get out of their misery."

Ultimately, said Father Chauveau, "When they cross the threshold of Magdalena House, I want them to feel accepted as they are; I want them to discover that despite their way of life, they are lovable."

You are precious in My sight, and honored, and I love you. (Isaiah 43:4)

May those who feel unworthy experience Your love, Lord.

'Stand in the Light of God's Grace'

Sam Haskell achieved great success in Hollywood as the Worldwide Head of Television with the William Morris Agency. And he attributes that success to the faith that his mother, Mary, taught him as a child.

During a "Christopher Closeup" interview, Haskell said, "I'm 66 years old, and I still think of what my mother told me as a five-year-old. She taught me that when the storms come, you get on your knees and pray for strength to endure. Or you pray for the mental capacity to help others get through it. You can pray in the shower or driving a car, but my mother thought the most important place to pray was on your knees.

"I would bring that to every situation I was involved with in Hollywood. It set an example that others wanted to follow, whether they were Christian, Jewish or agnostic. My mother used to say to me as a little boy, 'You go stand in the light of God's grace, and you show people who you really are, and they will respond. Do not hide in the shadows or the darkness. You stand in the light.' And that's what I've always tried to do."

Let us walk in the light of the Lord. (Isaiah 2:5)

Give me the courage to spread the light of Your love, Jesus.

Stress as a Spice of Life?

Stress is a part of life. It can be anything which upsets our equilibrium. The cause may be pleasant or painful. A marriage is stressful, but so too is a loved one's death.

According to Dr. Hans Selye, author of "Stress Without Distress," stress can be good, possibly even the spice of life. "Since stress is associated with all types of activity," he says, "we could avoid most of it only by never doing anything...Who would enjoy a life of no runs, no hits, no errors?"

So the goal isn't to avoid all stress but rather to learn to manage and control it to the extent possible. We naturally have the fight or flight reaction. But there are other choices.

In a Christopher News Note on the topic, experts suggest we can learn to gauge our responses. Psychiatrist Thomas F. Fogarty advises, "Seek a balance that realistically faces the possibilities, takes action as needed, and accepts what cannot be changed."

Can any of you by worrying add a single hour to your span of life? (Luke 12:25)

Help me, Holy Spirit, to understand the difference between stress and distress.

A Touchdown Pass in Generosity

Geno Smith, the quarterback for the New York Jets football team, had a rough start to the 2015 season, but he did his best to make the most of the year. Smith, who was decked by another Jets player (who was later fired) in a locker room brawl, broke his jaw and went through a lengthy rehab period. However, that didn't put a stop to his charitable activities.

According to New York's *Daily News,* Smith, who wears number seven for the Jets, gave seven youngsters from the Boys and Girls Club a special memory for the team's seven home games. Each of them would receive two tickets to a game, special club passes, an autographed jersey and other Jets memorabilia, and even a postgame meet-and-greet with Smith.

The mother of Khalliq Smith, one of the first youngsters honored, said the event made quite an impression on him. "Today was the first day I saw my son's eyes without sadness since his father passed," she smiled. "An absolutely priceless moment to share with him."

Open your hand to the poor and needy neighbor in your land. (Deuteronomy 15:11)

Let me take the opportunity to dispel someone's sadness today, Jesus.

Bowling for Dollars

When Michael Pressler wanted to find a charity to benefit from a fundraiser he'd planned, he didn't have far to look. His grandmother, who had died a short time before, always sent whatever she could to St. Jude Children's Research Hospital in Memphis, Tennessee.

Michael, then a student at Pequannock Township High School in New Jersey, decided that's where he wanted his money to go. He enlisted the help of his dad and the T-Bowl Bowling Center in nearby Wayne, and their mission was off and running.

Pressler signed up about 75 bowlers and together they raised some $2,400—not bad, but there was clearly a ways to go. Now, four years later, he got his fellow students at William Paterson University in Wayne to enroll their friends, and some 350 registrants raised more than $16,000 for the hospital.

Gene Myers helped spread the word by writing about it in *Suburban Trends,* a local newspaper, and plans are already under way—with a good four or five months' planning ahead—for next year's event.

Give, and it will be given to you. (Luke 6:38)

Holy Spirit, fill me with the desire to give generously.

The Heroic Chaplain of Vietnam

Among the hundreds of worshipers at the annual Memorial Mass for Father Vincent Capodanno, hero-chaplain of Vietnam, was a former Marine corporal who had known him in the last moments of his life. Raymond Harton, now of Carrollton, Georgia, lay wounded on a battlefield nearly 50 years ago.

Father Capodanno, then a Navy lieutenant, ran to his side in the midst of a firefight with the North Vietnamese. "He cupped the back of my head," the Georgia man recalled, "and said, 'Stay calm, Marine. Someone will be here to help us soon. God is with us all here today.'"

Those might have been his last words. As reported by *Salute,* the magazine of the Archdiocese for the Military Services, USA, he went to help another wounded Marine, and then both men were instantly killed by machine-gun fire. The story notes that Father Capodanno, whose chaplaincy was heroic in many ways, was posthumously awarded the Medal of Honor. The Church has named him a Servant of God and is considering his cause for canonization.

His heart was courageous in the ways of the Lord. (2 Chronicles 17:6)

Help all military chaplains serve courageously, Father.

Hot Under the Blue Collar

If there's one thing that makes TV host Mike Rowe hot under the collar, it's the suggestion that blue-collar jobs are somehow less important than white-collar work.

As he told Forbes.com, "Learning how to weld, or how to run electric, or how to install a toilet—these skills can and often do lead to fulfilling careers, balanced lives, and better than average pay....Studies show that welders pay off student loans a lot faster than baristas."

In addition, says Rowe, blue-collar work often leads to entrepreneurship: "Someone starts by mastering a trade, works hard, and begins to prosper. Then they decide to start their own business. They buy their own vans. They hire their own people. They create opportunity not just for themselves, but for the thousands of others who are literally keeping our lights on and our toilets flushing and our indoor temperature just the way we like it. Skills lead to careers, but they also lead to real businesses, and real prosperity. We forget that at our peril."

In all toil there is profit, but mere talk leads only to poverty. (Proverbs 14:23)

Guide the unemployed toward good opportunities, Lord.

Beautiful Threads of Grace

Best-selling author and *EWTN* host Donna-Marie Cooper O'Boyle exudes calm and grace, so discovering some of the ordeals she's had to endure throughout her life—from sexual assault to an alcoholic husband to physical and emotional abuse—comes as a surprise. She's got every reason to be cynical or angry, yet she remains a person filled with hope and faith.

The reason for that is implied in the title of O'Boyle's book, "The Kiss of Jesus: How Mother Teresa and the Saints Helped Me to Discover the Beauty of the Cross." O'Boyle personally knew Mother Teresa, and their friendship continues to impact her approach to life.

During a "Christopher Closeup" interview, O'Boyle admitted that it's not easy to see grace in times of suffering. It's only in retrospect that she saw the "beautiful threads of grace woven through" her life. Now, she simply trusts that God's graces are guiding her, even when she can't see or feel them. She adds, "We need to offer up all of our prayers, works, joys and sufferings, and ask our Lord to use them for His glory."

We have all received, grace upon grace. (John 1:16)

Open my eyes to the graces around me, Divine Messiah.

Smiles Are on the House at the Shack

"I want to personally challenge moms to believe in their child, no matter what society tells you." So says Mary Ann Pyron—and she should know. When her son Blake was born with Down Syndrome, people told her there were many things he wouldn't be able to do. Now, 20-year-old Blake has grown up to become the youngest business owner in Sanger, Texas.

As reported by *ABC News*, Blake worked at a local barbecue restaurant through his senior year of high school, but it wound up closing. Job opportunities in general—and for special needs people in particular—were not plentiful in Sanger, so the Pyrons looked into Blake starting his own business: a snow cone shack. With the community's support and help from family and friends, Blake's Snow Shack was born, giving the young man an outlet for his friendly personality. He said, "Smiles are always on the house at the Shack."

Mary Ann adds, "We were told Blake wouldn't be able to do things, and we looked past that. You don't know our child, so don't label him. We haven't, and he turned out great."

**I am fearfully and wonderfully made.
(Proverbs 139:14)**

Prevent me from labeling people, Lord, so I can see them as Your beloved children.

Two Hostages Hold on to Faith

Considering that Amanda Berry and Gina DeJesus were kidnapped, held hostage, abused, and sexually assaulted by Cleveland school bus driver Ariel Castro for 10 years, it might seem odd that they named the memoir about their experiences "Hope." But that is the word that perfectly describes these two young women who survived their darkness by relying on their faith in God and the light that was brought into their lives by Amanda's daughter Jocelyn, a child of her rape by Castro.

During an interview on "Christopher Closeup," the book's co-authors—Pulitzer Prize-winning journalists Mary Jordan and Kevin Sullivan—said, "Amanda found a little candle with a picture of Jesus on it in the basement, and she would light it and pray. It became a source of strength and hope for her."

Jocelyn's birth gave the girls a new and innocent life on which to focus, and helped stir up their determination to break free of their captor. When they finally escaped in 2013, one of the first things Gina did was go to church and light a candle for all the other missing girls in the world.

Set me free and rescue me. (Psalm 144:7)

Hear the cries of Your children who suffer captivity and assault, Savior.

An Actor's Platform for Good

Actor David Oyelowo, who starred as Rev. Martin Luther King Jr. in the Christopher Award-winning film "Selma," carefully chooses the movies in which he works. The reason? As he explained during a "Christopher Closeup" interview:

"I take very seriously the fact that the industry I'm in and what I do for a living impacts how people see the world. It shows them worlds that they haven't seen and educates them. But a lot of the time what we see on our screens are films or TV shows that leave you feeling no hope for humanity, or that glamorize violence or the lack of morality.

"For me, I have a moral compass that is very much shaped by my faith, but also by being a father and, I hope, a socially responsible citizen. I've seen films I've been involved with have a huge impact on culture: 'Selma,' for instance. I've seen it bring hope to people...That's something I feel privileged to be a part of. I want to continue using whatever platform I have to bring a degree of positivity to the world around me."

From everyone to whom much has been given, much will be required. (Luke 12:48)

Guide me in adding positivity to the world, Holy Spirit.

Marriage Isn't an Island

When a couple gets engaged, the focus would seem to fall on the two of them planning their life together. But as *Verily* magazine Relationships Editor Monica Gabriel discovered when she announced her engagement to Joe Marshall on Facebook, community is also a big part of the equation.

During a "Christopher Closeup" interview, Gabriel said, "A lot of people may think that marriage is an island, but I think most married couples will tell you this is untrue. It [involves] those around you who support you during the difficult times of marriage. They're also the people who get you *to* marriage.

"Looking at my own life, all of my friends [and family] were the people who were teaching me how to love. They will continue to teach me [when] I run across issues and I don't know how to talk to Joe about them. I'll run to my mom, or my sisters, or my friends. It's all those people who are rooting for you that help your marriage grow and thrive. Obviously, there's certain boundaries, but marriage is so important to our communities, I think it's something that we need to remember."

Provoke one another to love and good deeds. (Hebrews 10:24)

Lead married couples to the support they need, Lord.

A Reason to Get Out of Bed

"They're my kids. I may not be their official mom, but I think they know I'm here for them if they need me."

So says Michel Haigh, an associate professor at the Penn State College of Communications, to *The Atlantic* about her approach to teaching and connecting with her students. That approach must be working since the alumni association gave her an award during the 2014-2015 school year.

Haigh hails from Hitchcock, South Dakota, a town of fewer than 100 people. Connecting with others on a campus the size of Penn State seemed daunting, but she was able to do it because she pursues success with commitment and determination—and she expects her students to do the same. By emphasizing and modeling hard work, she hopes her "kids" become successful both personally and professionally.

Haigh concludes, "You should get out of bed wanting to make the world a better place. I get out of bed in the morning wanting to make sure that I'm doing something for my students."

I will instruct you and teach you the way you should go. (Psalm 32:8)

May all teachers be role models for their students, Father.

Patriotism at Ground Zero

New York *Daily News* sports radio-TV columnist Bob Raissman tossed a rare accolade in the direction of the NFL's Dallas Cowboys during the 2015 football season when he praised the Dallas coach for an unscheduled act of patriotism.

Raissman, who regularly reports on the New York Jets and the New York Giants, arch-rivals of the Dallas team, had welcome words of congratulations for an "exemplary decision" of Jason Garrett, the Dallas team's coach.

NFL coaches follow precise schedules and rarely deviate from them, Raissman explained. But when Garrett took his team to Ground Zero leading up to a game with the Giants, he showed not only a respect for all victims of the 9-11 tragedy, "but an understanding of the impact the visit would have on his players."

In awarding Garrett his "Dude of the Week" acclamation, Raissman concluded: "This was an experience they will never forget."

In the memory of virtue is immortality. (Wisdom 4:1)

Help me remember and share the example of the virtuous ones who rest in Your hands, Father.

The Smile That Changed the World

John Schlimm, Christopher Award-winning author of the memoir "Five Years in Heaven," is also an artist who created a project called "The Smile That Changed the World." It was inspired by his father who would always smile and wave at people as he was driving past them in his car.

One day, Schlimm asked him, "Who was that?" His dad answered that he didn't know the person. So why was he waving and smiling, Schlimm wanted to know. His dad's response: "The quickest way to make a friend is to smile at a stranger."

During a "Christopher Closeup" interview, Schlimm said, "Suddenly it clicked in my head: that's the power of a smile. Certainly, Mother Teresa has a great line about how a smile is the beginning of peace. So I developed a participatory art piece."

On a white canvas, Schlimm paints circles with eyes, then invites others to paint their own smiles into each one. Response has been positive. He said, "It's about people realizing that they themselves, through something as simple as a smile, have the power to change this world for the better."

A glad heart makes a cheerful countenance. (Proverbs 15:13)

Help me to make friends of strangers, Jesus.

How Does This DVD Player Work?

In her book "Senior Moments: Prayer-talks with God," Bernadette McCarver Snyder takes a humorous look at some of the challenges of aging and keeping up with modern technology.

Snyder laments the fact that her DVD player "keeps spitting out discs" because she pushed the wrong button; that her refrigerator's ice maker pops "out cubes late at night," making it sound like a robber broke into her house; and that her "new security system shrieks to high heaven if anyone touches a door or window."

And so she prays: "Help me, Lord, to be willing to try to learn about this new world. It can be embarrassing to feel so stupid about things even children take for granted. It can be depressing to even take notes about what to do and then still do it wrong. But, Lord, it has taken me a lifetime trying to learn about Your world of mysteries and miracles, and I'm still taking notes and studying and paying attention and rejoicing at every new little bit You reveal to me. So thank You, Lord, for being patient with me and for being such a good teacher."

The ear of the wise seeks knowledge. (Proverbs 18:15)

May I always be open to learning new things, Creator.

Seeing the Face of Jesus

In 2014, John Fawley was listening to "Christopher Closeup" on Relevant Radio in Wisconsin when he heard an interview with Chicago doctor Kevin Hunt, co-founder of the charity Medical Aid to Northern Uganda (MANU). Fawley got in touch with the group to ask if they could use the skills he developed as a volunteer first responder. They welcomed him to the team and made a medical mission trip to Uganda in 2016.

Fawley took blood pressures, did blood screenings, and performed other tasks. But his biggest takeaway from the experience was seeing the face of Jesus.

During a "Christopher Closeup" interview, he said, "The work we do seems very little in the scope of things, but if we help one person, we've done our job. We went to an orphanage for a day. Those Sisters there, they're the real heroes of the world. [I saw Jesus in] a little boy with smallpox hanging onto his piece of corn like it was the last piece of food; the 10-year-old girl with renal failure... I also saw the face of Jesus in Dr. Hunt [and the other team members]. It was an incredible trip."

Whoever sees Me sees Him who sent Me. (John 12:44)

Open my eyes to Your presence in this world, Jesus.

POW/MIA Recognition Day

Ninety-one-year-old Raymond Kooman of Little Ferry, New Jersey, celebrated POW/MIA Recognition Day in fine fashion. The World War II Army sergeant, taken prisoner himself during the famed Battle of the Bulge, was the guest of honor as 150 of his friends and neighbors took part in Bergen County's celebration of the day. Todd South of *The Record* explained that since 1979, the holiday has been observed on the third Friday of September each year.

Captured near Bastogne, Belgium, in December 1944, Kooman was taken to a prison camp where he slept on the floor and made do with one slice of bread a day. His weight, once a solid 160 pounds, dwindled down to half that. He and the other prisoners buried 50 or more of their fellow soldiers each week.

But there were happier times ahead. Kooman was liberated in April of 1945, and spent time in a hospital in England before returning to the U.S. His grandson had never heard the story of the older man's WWII service until that day. "Grandpa and I have a lot to catch up on," the young man declared.

He...broke their bonds asunder. (Psalm 107:14)

Bring peace to the families of those who never returned home from war, Divine Healer.

Serving the Aged Lovingly Today

A ministry for elders helps the young women who provide it grow in their faith—and at the same time offers a valuable service for the elderly. Known as SALT—Serving the Aged Lovingly Today—the program was arranged by the Carmelite Sisters for the Aging and Infirm in Germantown, New York.

As reported by Katie Scott of *Catholic News Service*, the young women who do the visiting keep in mind that they're providing pastoral care, not just making a social visit. "Some of the people we see don't have a lot of visitors," said one of the volunteers. And because many are near the end of their life span, "they are often more inclined to reflect on the past."

By putting life in perspective, the elderly often demonstrate a deep peace about things. "And that," said the volunteer, "is an amazing gift."

Your old men shall dream dreams and your young men shall see visions. (Joel 2:28)

Holy Spirit, lead me to learn from those who are older than I am—and from those who are younger, too.

Pope Francis Urges Forgiveness

When Pope Francis visited the United States, he made a huge impression on people of all faiths and on those of no apparent faith. Perhaps one of his most poignant impacts was on prisoners, particularly those he saw at the Curran-Fromhold Correctional Facility in Pennsylvania.

"Life is a journey, along different roads, different paths, which leave their mark on us," the pope said. He added that Jesus "doesn't ask us where we have been, He doesn't question us about what we have done....to all of us He stretches out a helping hand."

The pope made a point of stating that none of us is perfect or without need of forgiveness. After he left, one of the inmates who was facing drug charges said, "I feel so good. God has changed my heart. After this visit, we have to do better...We can't go back to doing things the same way."

Turn back to the Lord and forsake your sins; pray in His presence and lessen your offense. (Sirach 17:25)

Comfort us, Lord, in the knowledge that despite our fears, our sins are forgiven if we ask for Your mercy.

Learning Whether You Know It or Not

A rebellious youngster was sent to the school principal because he refused to do any homework. "I don't want to learn anything," the boy protested.

"Son, that's not the point," responded the principal. "You're learning something every day whether you know it or not. The question is, whether you're learning the right thing or the wrong thing."

No one ever stands still. We either go forward or backward, getting a little better or a little worse. By the same token, if we are not doing anything constructive to apply divine love and truth to an upset world, we are giving comfort and support, by default, to negative forces.

Check yourself frequently to make sure that you are acting positively for the glory of God and the best interests of mankind. We each have a responsibility to light candles rather than curse the darkness.

Whoever is not with Me is against Me, and whoever does not gather with Me scatters. (Luke 11:23)

Remind me, Holy Spirit, that by doing nothing I can actually cause harm.

Stuff: It's What's for Dinner

Have you ever eaten "Stuff" for dinner? Chances are you haven't because Jake Frost's mom is the one who invented it.

In *Catholic Digest,* he recalled that he and his siblings didn't know what to make of his mother's self-proclaimed Stuff at first, but they found it "inviting, even tantalizing...We ate it all, and we were licking our plates clean when the last bite of Stuff was gone. I still don't know what it was—a cornbread, goulash, meat-loafy hybrid—but it was good."

It was so good, they asked her to make it again. Only she couldn't. She said, "I don't know exactly how I made it or what I put into it...I don't think I could re-create it again."

And so, the now-adult Frost laments the loss of Stuff to history. But he sees a life lesson in it as well: "Some of life's best meals come when we aren't following our recipes, and some of life's best moments come when we aren't following our scripts. That's when we are dining at God's roadside canteen, where the food is always spicy, and following God's storyline instead of our own."

Eat what is offered to you. (Ezekiel 3:1)

Help me to appreciate life's unexpected joys, Father.

When God Doesn't Fix It

Two years after singer-songwriter Laura Story got married, her husband Martin was diagnosed with a brain tumor that required risky surgery. Martin survived, but he experienced major short-term memory loss. Though it has improved in the ensuing years, it remains an issue—and likely always will.

This experience has taught Laura a lot about faith. During a "Christopher Closeup" interview about her book "When God Doesn't Fix It," she said, "Believers can face disappointments, [but we can] work them out by leaning on our faith. We have to choose whether to evaluate God based on our circumstances—or choose to evaluate our circumstances based on what we've always [believed] about God. If we choose the latter, it's saying, 'God, I'm going to trust You in the valleys.'

"Scripture talks about joy that we can have despite our circumstances. It's not wrong to pray for a change in circumstances. I pray that my husband will receive healing. And right after that, I say, 'Okay, God, will You open my eyes to the opportunities we have today in the midst of the waiting?'"

The Lord is near to the brokenhearted. (Psalm 34:18)

Lord, help me find opportunities in times of trouble.

A Welcoming Family

Many years ago, there was a young boy—the grandson of slaves—born into poverty in New Orleans. As if that wasn't difficult enough, his father abandoned the family and his mother became a prostitute to support her children.

This boy had a gift for music and often sang in the streets so that passersby would give him money. But more importantly, at age seven, he befriended a Jewish family named Karnofsky, who had immigrated to the U.S. from Lithuania. They had pity on him and offered him some work in their home.

The Karnofskys treated this boy with kindness, and he came to live with them for a while. At bedtime, Mrs. Karnofsky would sing him a Russian lullaby, and he would learn to sing and play songs from their heritage. They even bought him his first musical instrument because they saw potential in him.

That boy grew up to be legendary jazz musician Louis Armstrong. He wore a Star of David around his neck all of his life as a tribute to his adopted Jewish family.

You shall also love the stranger, for you were strangers in the land of Egypt. (Deuteronomy 10:19)

Open my heart to making friends of strangers, Father.

From Fear to Faith

During hard times, when we need to pray with great faith and trust, it would help to imitate the prophet Habakkuk. Here is the historical setting:

It was the height of the Babylonian power some 600 years before Jesus. Habakkuk's nation had been overrun. Most of its people had been deported into slavery. Famine stalked the land.

Yet Habakkuk prayed: "Though the fig does not blossom, and no fruit is on the vines; though the produce of the olive fails and the fields yield no food; though the flock is cut off from the fold and there is no herd in the stalls, yet I will rejoice in the Lord. I will exult in the God of my salvation." (Habakkuk 3:17-18)

Pray to have a little of Habakkuk's trust! And remember that God will never desert you.

The earth will be filled with the knowledge of the glory of the Lord as the waters cover the sea. (Habakkuk 2:14)

Trust. Belief. Knowledge of Your glory. Whatever I call it, Lord, increase my trust, my belief, my knowledge of You.

Serving the Untouchables

When American-born nun Sister Annie Credidio moved to Ecuador in the mid-1980s to be a teacher at El Nuevo Mundo School, she attended Mass at a local hospital and noticed that members of the congregation were missing fingers, toes, legs, and teeth. She soon discovered that this was a hospital for people with Hansen's Disease (also known as leprosy).

The more she explored the facility and talked to patients, the more she realized how deplorable conditions were. With the full support of her order—the Sisters of Charity of the Blessed Virgin Mary—she gave up her teaching job to create a better life for those society deemed "the untouchables."

She cleaned up the facility, brought compassion and better treatment to the patients, and co-founded a foundation called Damien House to make sure their needs were always taken care of. During an interview on "Christopher Closeup," Sister Annie said, "I really do believe that God taps us on the shoulder and puts us where we need to be when the time is right."

**Cure the sick...cleanse the lepers.
(Matthew 10:8)**

Help me to show compassion to society's "untouchables," Lord.

If God Wants...

Sister Annie Credidio has changed the lives of the patients with Hansen's Disease (a.k.a. leprosy) that she cares for in Ecuador's Damien House, but they have transformed her life and faith as well. Despite feeling abandoned by their families and society, these people never lost their belief that God was watching over them.

During an interview on "Christopher Closeup," Sister Annie recalled, "They would always say, *'Si Dios quiere*—if God wants' and *'la voluntad de Dios,'* the will of God.' I thought, 'Wow, these people are always mentioning God.'

"So many of them needed amputations, they needed eye surgery, they were losing their teeth. Yet they say, 'If God wants.' Their spirituality shook me...I thought I knew what faith was about, but I found out that true faith is letting everything go and letting God take over."

Trust in Him at all times, O people; pour out your heart before Him; God is a refuge for us. (Psalm 62:8)

In times of sickness, struggle, or disappointment, Father, I find it difficult to believe in Your goodness. Help me build up my faith and trust in You.

Purlettes Sew Up Investment

In 2005, Sarah Oliver of Mill Valley, California, started designing and knitting handbags for family and friends. They became so popular that she started selling them at trunk shows. With demand for increased production, she knew she wanted to hire people to do the work here in the United States, but she had to find an economical option.

Oliver approached The Redwoods Senior Retirement Community in her area to see if any knitters were interested in working with her. Response was positive and a new business—Sarah Oliver Handbags—was born. The business even got an investment on the TV series "Shark Tank."

Oliver's elderly knitters call themselves "The Purlettes + 1" because of their "knit one, purl two" expertise and the fact that they're full of pearls of wisdom. The + 1 represents the only male knitter, Hector. Their average age is 88, and their shared purpose gives them a strong sense of community. Daphne, age 93, says, "Being a Purlette is the joy of my elder life."

Gray hair is a crown of glory; it is gained in a righteous life. (Proverbs 16:31)

Inspire our culture to appreciate our elders, Holy Spirit.

Where the Mentally Afflicted Find a Home

The Belgian town of Geel has a special place in its heart for St. Dymphna, patroness of the mentally ill. According to legend, the saint—a 7th-century Irish princess—was killed there by her maddened father after she tried to flee from him. A 14th-century church houses Dymphna's remains.

But the people of Geel do not just welcome the saint. For centuries, they have opened their homes to those who seek her intercession. According to a report by *NPR's* Angus Chen, people with a wide range of mental illnesses and disabilities, some of them severe, live with the people of Geel in their homes, not as patients but as beloved guests.

"Boarders tend to stay in family care for years," Chen writes. "In some cases, when boarders' caretakers grow too old or die, they continue to live with their caretakers' children." Today there are some 250 boarders living in Geel, sheltered by a rare and centuries-old hospitality.

Do not neglect to show hospitality to strangers, for by doing that some have entertained angels. (Hebrews 13:2)

Lord Jesus, remind me that when I welcome the stranger, I welcome You.

Newlywed Sees God in His Wife

The "in sickness and in health" marriage vow became a reality much sooner than expected for newlyweds Matt and Nell Weber. A few months after their wedding, Matt experienced a debilitating stomach problem that required life-saving surgery.

It was a trying time, but Matt gained a new perspective on his relationship with God that is tied to his bond with Nell. During a "Christopher Closeup" interview about his book "Operating on Faith: A Painfully True Love Story," he said:

"My wife is my heart and my soul. She's everything that I think is good with the world. In many ways, it's easy to pray to Jesus and have that relationship when you're sick and in need. But not everyone sees that in the caretaker—in your wife—in all the things that they do for you. That person is living out the words and deeds of Jesus Christ. My relationship with God was strengthened in that I saw [Him] and everything that we hear in the Gospel played out in my wife's words and deeds. It was this new way of experiencing God through this new vow that I had taken with my wife."

Husbands, love your wives, just as Christ loved the church. (Ephesians 5:25)

Help husbands and wives practice sacrificial love, Lord.

What's In a Name

In the 19th century, Leopold von **Asphalt,** a wealthy Bavarian landlord, developed a mixture of tar, pitch and sand for paving roads.

The stage collapsed during Alessandro **Fiasco's** production of the opera, *Lucia di Lamermoor,* in Mantua, Italy. Imre **Kiosk** owned over 400 stalls selling newspapers and cigarettes throughout the late 19th century Austro-Hungarian Empire.

An Argentine botanist, Jorge **Avocado,** introduced that ovoid green staple of guacamole to Europe. The first to boil oranges with sugar was João **Marmalado** in 15th century Portugal. Poet Emily **Satchel's** poems may not be familiar to us now, but her tote bag is.

These words are eponyms, which means the items are named after the people who discovered them, invented them, or made them popular. Honor the uniqueness behind the name of every human being you meet.

A good name is to be chosen rather than great riches. (Proverbs 22:1)

Jesus, help me grow into the unique person I was created to be.

Caregiving Leads to Compassion

Over a period of 14 years, Emily and Jennifer Houle watched their grandparents suffer through Alzheimer's and other ailments—and sometimes they assisted their mom Marcy in caring for them. While some people felt sorry that the girls had to deal with so much illness, Marcy believes it turned them into stronger, more compassionate people.

Both Emily and Jennifer went on to become doctors, and noted that their caregiving experiences taught them to not just treat patients as a collection of symptoms, but as human beings who require patience and compassion.

During a "Christopher Closeup" interview about her book "The Gift of Caring," Marcy also explained that while being a caregiver can be very stressful, she ultimately sees it as a gift, not a burden, because she was "able to give back to the people that I loved, who'd taken care of me and loved me." In addition, her Catholic faith brought her "the strength I needed. God was at my side and my family was at my side, and we still had that love."

Let us not grow weary in doing what is right. (Galatians 6:9)

Awaken compassion in my heart for all who suffer, Father.

The World's Oldest Living Man

Born in Poland, Israel Kristal lived through two World Wars and even made it out of the Auschwitz concentration camp. Tragically, his first wife, Chaya, and their two children did not survive Auschwitz.

Five years after the conclusion of World War II, Kristal immigrated to Haifa, Israel, with his second wife and their son, Heim. There, he ran a thriving confectionary business until his retirement. He now enjoys the simple pleasures of life, which includes being a proud great-grandparent!

As of March 11, 2016, according to Guinness World records, Kristal was given the title the "world's oldest living man," at 112 years of age and 178 days, respectively. "I don't know the secret for long life," he stated upon receiving his Guinness World's record certificate. "I believe everything is determined from above and we shall never know the reasons why. There have been smarter, stronger and better-looking men than me who are no longer alive. All that is left for us to do is to keep on working as hard as we can."

With long life I will satisfy them, and show them My salvation. (Psalm 91:16)

Abba, may we always respect and learn from our elders.

'Wherever We Are, God Is!'

"Everything is grace." Those words of St. Thérèse of Lisieux (a.k.a. The Little Flower) were spoken when she was dying of tuberculosis and experiencing a long spiritual darkness. Yet she chose to believe in God's love anyway, a remarkable act of faith. Father Bob Colaresi, O. Carm., Director of the Society of the Little Flower, recently endured the darkness of prostate cancer so he writes about this view of grace:

"St. Thérèse's greatest teaching is a challenge to look for and see that God is everywhere...The flip side of that biblical teaching is that wherever we are, God is! Yes, wherever we are physically, mentally, emotionally, spiritually, and relationally, God is with us—present within our experience.

"God is often hidden within our human experiences, as He was throughout our biblical history, clouded in mystery, yet truly present! We simply have to open our eyes and listen with our heart...What are the dark nights of your life and our world teaching you?"

The faithful will abide with Him in love, because grace and mercy are upon His holy ones. (Wisdom 3:9)

Give me the vision to see Your grace everywhere, Jesus.

The Prodigal at the Bus Depot

It was a hot October day when Deacon Chip Wilson from the Diocese of Charlotte, North Carolina, arrived at the local bus depot to pick up a friend. That's when he noticed a teenage girl sitting on a bench. She had multiple tattoos and facial piercings, wore a buttoned-up trenchcoat, and looked scared.

She asked to borrow his cell phone, explaining that she had traveled 17 hours from Ohio for a surprise visit to her grandparents. Their meeting hadn't gone well, but she wanted to call them. Deacon Wilson knew she had nowhere else to go.

He had started searching for homeless shelters on his smartphone in case he needed to offer help. But the girl's grandmother pulled up in her car and ran out to embrace the girl.

They each apologized to the other, and the girl unbuttoned her coat, revealing a baby bump. Writing on the website Aleteia, Deacon Wilson said he believed the grandmother might leave. Instead, "Grandma knelt, wrapped her arms around that belly and kissed it." Deacon Wilson saw the scene as God's love in action.

His father saw him and was filled with compassion; he ran...and kissed him. (Luke 15:20)

May I be humble enough to practice mercy, Lord.

A Veteran's Fight, A Judge's Heart (Part One)

Special Forces Green Beret Joe Serna had witnessed and endured some horrific times during his three tours of duty in Afghanistan. Not only did he lose a lot of friends there, but he suffered injuries in a suicide bombing that forced him to retire.

Depression and bad decisions followed, including driving while impaired. Diagnosed with post-traumatic stress disorder (PTSD), he entered a veteran's treatment court program in Fayetteville, North Carolina. But Serna's struggles continued.

When he stood before Judge Lou Olivera on April 12, 2016, Serna lied about a urinalysis test that came back positive. Eventually, he admitted the truth, so Judge Olivera had no choice but to send him to jail for one day.

But the judge was a combat veteran himself and knew that this incident could trigger Serna's PTSD. That's when he decided to do something unusual. As reported by the *Fayetteville Observer*, Judge Olivera spent the night in jail with Serna.

The rest of the story tomorrow.

I was in prison and you visited Me. (Matthew 25:36)

Help me ease someone's burdens, Merciful Savior.

A Veteran's Fight, A Judge's Heart (Part Two)

Joe Serna was sitting on the bunk in his cell when Judge Lou Olivera walked in to spend the night with him. Serna told Bill Kirby Jr. of the *Fayetteville Observer*, "I knew this was a very compassionate man. I know how involved he is with veterans, and he's a veteran himself."

Serna and Olivera talked for hours about their lives, families, and military service. It made a difference. Serna stated, "I look at him as a father...I will never let him down again."

Explaining his own motivation, Judge Olivera said: "I thought about a story I once read. It talked about a soldier with PTSD in a hole. A family member, a therapist, and a friend all throw down a rope to help the veteran suffering. Finally, a fellow veteran climbs into the hole with him. The soldier suffering with PTSD asks, 'Why are you down here?' The fellow veteran replied, 'I am here to climb out with you.'"

Two are better than one, because they have a good reward for their toil. For if they fall, one will lift up the other. (Ecclesiastes 4:9-10)

May we as individuals and as a country support our veterans in times of need, Prince of Peace.

Colbert vs. Maher

When avowed atheist Bill Maher appeared on the talk show of practicing Catholic Stephen Colbert, the conversation turned to religion when the host brought it up.

Colbert noted that Maher had been raised Catholic and then invited him back to the Church. He said, "Come on back, Bill. The door is always open. All you have to do is humble yourself before the presence of the Lord and admit that there are things greater than you in the universe that you do not understand. Then, salvation awaits you."

Colbert then asked Maher to take Pascal's Wager, which suggests that people should behave as if God exists and see if their lives change and belief develops.

Unfortunately, Maher would have none of it, and continued to insult the beliefs of Christianity. Still, it was a rare occasion in which a celebrity like Colbert humbly shared his faith in front of millions of television viewers. He may not have swayed his guest, but maybe he planted other seeds in the process.

Go into all the world and proclaim the good news to the whole creation. (Mark 16:15)

Help me to humbly and courageously share my faith in loving ways, Jesus.

The 'Boy's Town Difference'

Joanna Musgrove was in a downward spiral, even though she was only 15. Eating disorders and addictions to drugs and alcohol controlled her life—and she even attempted suicide. Her parents were shocked by the turn their daughter's life had taken. Thankfully, they connected Joanna with child-behavior experts at Boy's Town, in Omaha, Nebraska, and that made all the difference.

Many people know Boy's Town because of its founder, Father Edward Flanagan, and the classic movie in which he was portrayed by Spencer Tracy. But the organization offers all "at-risk children and families the love, support and education they need to succeed."

Under the care of Licensed Mental Health Counselor Rebekah Chillemi, Joanna was able to get and stay sober by her 18th birthday. She holds a job and plans to finish high school. Her relationship with her parents and sister has also improved. She now wants to be a role model for her younger sister after being a bad influence in the past: "I want to be a hero to her."

My help comes from the Lord. (Psalm 121:2)

Lord, I accept the responsibility of being a role model.

A Former Addict, a Holy Life

When Father Bill Kottenstette died in 2015 in Kirksville, Missouri, students at Truman State University there mourned him for many reasons. Father Bill, who had been chaplain at Truman's Newman Center for 19 years, was a great listener and had an endearing, goofy sense of humor. He also understood life's struggles because he'd endured many himself.

Father Kottenstette began drinking as a Jesuit seminarian, hiding his problem well enough to be ordained in 1973. When a doctor prescribed Valium as part of his treatment, he became addicted to that as well.

Released from the Jesuits in order to focus on his recovery, his addictions spun out of control. Finally, at age 47, he took a bus to Kirksville, where a sister lived. He found hospitality at a rectory there, followed the 12-step program of Alcoholics Anonymous, and once more took up his vocation.

"What I miss most about him," a student said, "is talking to him about all the good things in my life." Father Bill appreciated those good things most of all.

Do not get drunk with wine...but be filled with the Spirit. (Ephesians 5:18)

Guide those struggling with addiction, Messiah.

The Heart of a Child

Grace Schaefer was only seven years old when she first learned about the tragedy of abortion after attending a Holy Hour for Life at her family's local Omaha, Nebraska church. Grace remarked that day, "These babies may be small, but they are people, too."

According to the diocesan newspaper *The Catholic Voice,* Grace's mother explained that women who opted for this choice did so because they were "scared" of being unable to care for their babies. The youngster immediately thought of a simple but surefire way to help these women—by making pillows.

Each pillow would bear the design of a swaddled baby against the backdrop of a cross. Particular emphasis would be placed on the image of the baby's heart, which would have rays of light shining from it.

Four years later, Grace's healing ministry, aptly named "Heart of a Child," is still going strong, having donated $16,000 of its pillow profits to local pro-life organizations, such as Bethlehem House and Essential Pregnancy Services.

Before I formed you in the womb I knew you. (Jeremiah 1:5)

Father, may we never undervalue the sanctity of life.

Change Your Thoughts, Change Your Life

Ralph Marston runs the website The Daily Motivator and loves sharing words of inspiration with his online followers. Here are his insights on the power of thoughts:

"Your thoughts are what frighten you. Choose to change them, and the fear is gone. Your thoughts are what cause you to be frustrated, angry, disappointed, impatient, and uncomfortable. And your thoughts can also take you far away from all those things. For your thoughts can transform anger into forgiveness, disappointment into determination, discomfort into inspiration, and fear into love. The choice is always yours.

"The world is what it is. Yet your thoughts determine how you situate yourself into the world...At the times when you realize it, and at the times when you don't, you are always controlling your thoughts. Deep inside you is a beautiful, unique person who seeks true joy and fulfillment. Let your thoughts resonate with the genuine person you are, and that joy does surely come."

Be transformed by the renewing of your minds. (Romans 12:2)

Guide me in turning my thoughts in a positive direction, Holy Spirit.

A Parishioner's Unexpected Gift

Priests often have to ask for money from the pulpit to meet church expenses, but Msgr. Theophilus Anthony Joseph of St. Ephrem Church in Dyker Heights, Brooklyn, made a most unusual request: he needed a kidney.

As reported by *WCBS-TV,* the priest had suffered with kidney disease for eight years and needed a transplant. But four potential donors turned out to be incompatible with him. He kept praying for help, but came to feel like God wasn't listening.

Msgr. Joseph finally decided to take a different approach at a healing service, addressing the congregation directly: "I was very funny about it. I said, 'Look, I need a kidney. You could give me one, lend me one, sell me one, but I need a kidney.'"

Parishioner Grace Kippling volunteered, even though she barely knew the priest. But she was a match and everything went smoothly. She said, "The first time I saw him again, and I saw the difference between when he had asked for the kidney and how he was now, I just started crying. It was incredible."

Do good...expecting nothing in return. Your reward will be great. (Luke 6:35)

May I give selflessly to others in small or large ways, Lord.

Don't Belittle Yourself

Katrina, a friend of The Christophers and regular listener to our radio show, was standing in line at the market one day when she heard a voice behind her say, "Boy, you are stupid!" Katrina turned around, but the woman quickly said, "I'm not talking to you. I was saying that to myself." Katrina wondered why this stranger would belittle herself in that manner.

Soon after, Katrina was listening to Relevant Radio when a guest suggested that the devil "wants us to see ourselves as damaged goods." He added that "we need to believe in the power and mercy of God to recreate us." Katrina then wrote several self-affirmations that could benefit those with low self-worth:

"God loves me, so I am free to love myself. I will find joy by surrendering to God's will in the present moment. I will feed my soul by nurturing someone who needs my time and attention. I trust God to bring peace to my heart and show me how to share that peace with others. God, who is my Light and Salvation, will shine His Light in my soul today."

What are human beings that You are mindful of them... You have crowned them with glory and honor. (Hebrews 2:6-7)

I take comfort in being Your child, Heavenly Father.

One Man Stops 64 Trains

It was the 1950s when 64 commuter trains, headed for New York City during the morning rush hour, were stopped by a hit-and-run driver. This man delayed 45,000 individuals by as much as thirty-five minutes on their way to work.

All the trouble started when the motorist crashed into a pole supporting telephone and telegraph cables at the side of the tracks. When the first pole toppled, the weight of the cables caused seven other poles to snap one by one. The falling cables landed on the third rail, causing a short circuit. To prevent further trouble, railway officials cut off the power on all four tracks. One man thus compelled 45,000 others to sit and wait.

What one person does—or fails to do—can have far reaching effects. The peace, happiness, and destiny of countless individuals is involved in what we do. We will not know until we stand before God how many people have been helped—or hurt—by what each of us thinks, says, and does.

The fruit of the righteous is a tree of life. (Proverbs 11:30)

Let me be so busy serving the best interests of others, Jesus, that I will never even risk harming them.

Unlikely Teachers for Reluctant Readers

Every school has reluctant readers—students who struggle with reading aloud and sounding out the more difficult words in a passage. In the second- and fourth-grade classes of Utica, New York's Notre Dame Elementary School, these students receive help from the unlikeliest but most effective of sources: Carlo, a one-year-old mini-schnauzer and Sophia, a five-year-old Yorkie.

Carlo and Sophia never rush or criticize their young pupils; they simply sit beside them and listen patiently as the children read. Sondra Nassar, Notre Dame's librarian who supervises these weekly sessions, notes the tremendous improvement in her students' oral and reading skills after only a few such lessons.

These canine companions also visit the younger grades of Notre Dame, teaching them about animals and lessening their fears about meeting dogs for the first time. "[The children] know that the dogs are non-judgmental and they won't be made fun of," Nassar concludes in *The Catholic Sun*. "You know dog spelled backwards is God, and He's non-judgmental, too."

Who teaches us more than the animals of the Earth, and makes us wiser? (Job 35:11)

God, protect our pets, life's guardians and teachers.

Vets Building Character in Kids

All over the country—from New Jersey to Wisconsin to California—a distinguished group of military veterans is carrying out one of its most important assignments: teaching youngsters to do the right thing. That's the goal of a group from the Congressional Medal Foundation, which is using its character development program to pass along to students how easy and rewarding it is to help others.

For example, in Covina, California, students collected supplies for homeless veterans—sheets, blankets and towels—and then discussed their work under the guidance of classroom teacher Sheila Edwards. "Kids need to know the words," she told Kathleen McCleary of *Parade* magazine. "When you're giving to others, that's sacrifice. Labeling it makes it powerful."

The Medal of Honor winners work with schools throughout the country to foster principles of effective character education in ways which improve academics, enhance student behavior, and generally make for a better school climate.

Character produces hope, and hope does not disappoint us. (Romans 5:4-5)

Help young people to build a strong and good moral foundation, Father.

A Prayer of Praise and Gratitude

St. Teresa of Ávila once wrote a litany of gratitude that reads in part: "May You be blessed forever, Lord, for not abandoning me when I abandoned You.

...for offering Your hand of love in my darkest, most lonely moment.

...for putting up with such a stubborn soul.

...for loving me more than I love myself.

...for continuing to pour out Your blessings though I respond so poorly.

...for drawing out the goodness in all people, even including me.

...for repaying our sin with Your love.

...for being constant and unchanging.

...for Your countless blessings on me and on all Your creatures."

Stand up and bless the Lord your God. (Nehemiah 9:5)

May all that is in me bless You, Merciful and Generous Lord.

A Happy Septic Tank Cleaner?

"The world is full of very happy septic-tank cleaners and miserable investment bankers," says Mike Rowe about approaching your work with a positive attitude. The former host of TV's "Dirty Jobs" told *National Review's* Ericka Andersen, "There's nothing magical about job satisfaction... It has much less to do with the job and everything to do with the person."

Rowe recalled someone leaving this story on his Facebook page: "I'm 30 and I've been miserable most of my working career...Then I saw an episode of 'Dirty Jobs' where you were cleaning chimneys, so I went to the National Chimney Sweep Cleaning Institute and got certified and now I've got two employees, a van and my own business."

Andersen concluded, "[Rowe] doesn't recommend that unhappy investment bankers quit their jobs and become chimney sweeps. However, someone coming out of high school or college—or locked into a dead-end job—shouldn't see a skilled trade as something beneath his intelligence or status. Many of these industries are hiring like crazy, and it's not difficult to get the training necessary to obtain one."

In all toil there is profit. (Proverbs 14:23)

Help me approach my job with a positive attitude, Creator.

Strawberry's Road Out of Darkness, Part One

Former Mets and Yankees slugger Darryl Strawberry became known as much for his drug and alcohol problems as his on-the-field play. But one of the most positive influences in Strawberry's life was his Mets teammate Gary Carter, with whom he played on the 1986 championship team. "He was the light in the darkness," Strawberry told *Newsday's* Jim Baumbach.

The 1986 Mets were known for their hard-partying ways, but Carter—a husband and father devoted to his Christian faith—never took part in those activities. In retrospect, Strawberry realized he was too immature to appreciate Carter's example.

He said, "I had an opportunity to see a man that I didn't see in my home...I didn't have a father figure. Deep down inside, I wanted to be a man that lived right, that didn't go out and drink, didn't cheat on your wife, didn't do drugs or drink alcohol."

Strawberry didn't turn his back on that lifestyle just yet, but Carter's example always stayed with him. More tomorrow.

Let your light shine before others. (Matthew 5:16)

Father, may I strive to set a positive example for others.

Strawberry's Road Out of Darkness, Part Two

Drugs, alcohol, rehab, and even domestic violence charges plagued Darryl Strawberry for years until he met his current wife Tracy, who helped him turn his life around. That was also the time that the seeds Gary Carter had planted in his life finally blossomed. Strawberry became an ordained minister and now shares his story with others in similar situations.

But in 2011, the unexpected happened. Carter was diagnosed with brain cancer, which led to his death at age 57. It was a shock to former teammates and fans alike that the clean-living Carter would meet his end so young.

Strawberry visited his mentor during his illness to tell him what his example had meant to him, and how much he appreciated the fact that he never judged him, even during Strawberry's darkest days.

As reported by *Newsday's* Jim Baumbach, Carter told his old friend, "I'm just overjoyed about your life." Strawberry recalled, "Hearing that made me understand I am doing it right."

Repent therefore, and turn to God so that your sins may be wiped out. (Acts 3:19)

Guide those with addiction problems into Your healing light, Lord.

'You Help Others and I'll Help You'

Among the flurry of last-minute audiences held by Pope Francis during his 2015 U.S. visit was one with Mary Jo Copeland of Minneapolis, founder of Sharing and Caring Hands in that city. She was accompanied by her husband, Dick, and Auxiliary Bishop Andrew Cozzens of St. Paul-Minneapolis to this meeting, held at the Vatican Embassy in Washington.

Copeland, 73, has been compared with Mother Teresa of Kolkata for her work with the poor. She and her husband raised 12 children of their own before she founded Sharing and Caring Hands, which provides a loving environment for previously-homeless men, women and children in downtown Minneapolis. Between the property and the facility itself, she spent several hundred thousand dollars of her own money on the facility.

She told Dave Hrbacek of *The Catholic Spirit,* "God says to me when I pray, 'You help others and I'll help you, Mary. You take care of My people and I'll take care of you.' And, He has. I think that's what God is saying through this visit."

Whoever is kind to the poor lends to the Lord, and will be repaid in full. (Proverbs 19:17)

Show me what I can do to help You, Lord.

Me, Worry?

Do you find yourself lying awake at night, or whiling away hours at work, worrying? Here are four tips to "kick the worrying habit:"

- **Keep a worry log.** Writing them down slows the process, and forces you to finish one worry before moving on to the next.
- **Set a time limit.** Worrying is an addictive habit. Control it and then kick it. Allot yourself a set amount of time each day to obsess and don't worry outside of that time frame.
- **Tune into negative thinking.** In your mind, play out your worst "what if" scenarios, and then ask yourself: "How likely is this?"
- **Let others take charge of their own lives.** The more you worry about others and their lives and problems, the less they feel responsible for their own actions and concerns. Spread the responsibility around a little!

Concern is useful, worry isn't. Give your troubles to God—His shoulders are stronger than yours.

> **Do not worry about your life...Do not worry about tomorrow. (Matthew 6:25,34)**

I turn my cares over to You, Lord, my strength, my consolation, my peace.

The Street Priest's Ministry

Before his death in 2012, Father John C. Flynn of the Bronx was known as a "street priest" throughout the New York Archdiocese, so it was altogether fitting that a section of a Bronx thoroughfare was renamed in his honor. A stretch of East 182nd Street will henceforth be known as John C. Flynn Way, and the crowd that gathered there for the ceremony voiced their enthusiastic approval.

Father Flynn was no ordinary priest, as David Gonzalez, who covered the renaming for *The New York Times,* made clear in his report. As pastor of St. Martin of Tours parish, Father Flynn "became famous for taking his ministry into the Bronx neighborhood of Crotona. When he despaired over saying funeral Masses for teenagers felled by drugs and gang violence, he took to the streets, offering to exchange a crucifix for a gun.

"It was symbolic, he admitted. But so, he said, was the cross that was at the center of his faith."

Those who are well have no need of a physician, but those who are sick...I have come not to call the righteous but sinners. (Matthew 9:12-13)

Jesus, send me out to serve those who need You most.

Listening is Communicating

There's an old proverb that says, "God gave us two ears and one mouth, so we ought to listen twice as much as we speak." Ironically, that advice could lead to people thinking of you as a great communicator!

Radio personality and author Earl Nightingale once had this to say about the subject of listening: "It's curious, but a fact nonetheless, that the best listeners are often considered by others to be marvelous conversationalists.

"In the hierarchy of human needs, recognition is number one. We don't recognize people by talking to them; we recognize them by listening to what they have to say, until they overdo it.

"Knowing when to speak and when to listen is a rather sensitive thing. It's just a matter of good manners. And there's nothing wrong with silence."

Truly God has listened; He has given heed to the words of my prayer. (Psalm 66:19)

Father, may I be as patient and compassionate a listener with others as You are with me.

A Coach Who Cares

By winning two Super Bowls, Tom Coughlin established his football legacy as coach of the New York Giants. His personal legacy is assured as well. He and his wife, Judy, have made a glittering success of the Jay Fund—named for a former player of Coughlin's at Boston College.

The Jay Fund was created when Jay McGillis died at the age of 22 after contracting leukemia while a member of the school's team, the Eagles. With permission from Jay's mom, Pat, the Coughlins launched the fund to aid families with children who have cancer. It has grown through Coughlin's subsequent coaching jobs in Jacksonville, Florida, and New York.

For instance, the Fund, which assists with family expenses, originally raised $36,000. By 2015, proceeds had swelled to $1.5 million. The coach added, "We're also there emotionally."

As Pat told Ron LaJoie of *Catholic New York,* "When Jay was diagnosed, Tom was there for the McGillis family. His love and compassion were endless."

Your words have supported those who were stumbling, and You have made firm the feeble knees. (Job 4:4)

May I be a support to those who are suffering, Divine Healer.

A Reminder From Heaven

Actor Maurice Johnson shared the following story on his Facebook page: "Today, as I was heading to the gym, I passed a car with its hood up. It was an older lady and she had this helpless look on her face. I backed up before entering the interstate and asked if she was okay.... She [told me] she had just bought a battery, but her car went dead at the light.

"I said, 'Ma'am, it's your alternator.' She said, 'You must be a country boy!' I jumped her car and advised her to go straight home instead of [finishing] her errands. I followed her home and the car cut off again, but I jumped it again until we got her car parked back at her apartment complex.

"After saying how long she'd been sitting in the road and unable to get anyone on the phone, it reminded me how different things are in this world today. I told her I grew up in a smaller city, but it was second nature for me to stop and make sure she was okay...I told her my name and she told me hers was Fannie. I said, 'Ms. Fannie, that was my grandmother's name and maybe she is reminding me to be a gentleman from heaven.'"

Let each of you look not to your own interests, but to the interests of others. (Philippians 2:4)

Inspire me to help someone on the road of life, Father.

The Cooking Priest

Father Leo Patalinghug has a delicious way of spreading the Gospel message, through one of his favorite and long-cherished hobbies: cooking. To that end, he hosts his own culinary show called "Savoring our Faith," which airs on the Eternal Word Television Network. He also travels across the nation holding workshops for people of all ages on "how food and faith meet."

This aptly-named "cooking priest" acknowledges his form of Christian ministry may be a bit unorthodox, but nevertheless, it has proven to be extremely effective. Father Leo references a touching email he received from a woman who, after watching one of his shows, was inspired to go to church, confess, and receive communion for the first time in 30 years.

"And I thought, I was just cutting onions, you know?" Father Leo marveled in his interview with *Catholic News Service*. "It's kind of crazy, but I was doing it in the name of the Lord…Once people nibble on the truth, once they've tasted and seen the goodness of God, they hunger for more."

One does not live by bread alone, but by every word that comes from the mouth of God. (Matthew 4:4)

God, may we always hunger and thirst for Your Holy Word.

The Big Picture of Prayer

During a conversation among young people in New York City, a study was mentioned that cited a connection between prayer and the improvement of critically ill patients. Both Willie, a student, and Bill, a police officer, expressed a belief in prayer's ability to heal.

Willie said, "I'm not really sure what it all means, but I know that when I pray, regularly, I feel better. I'm not sure about physically, but...I can't explain it. I feel happier."

"It's a sense of peace," Bill explained. "For people who pray, no matter what else goes wrong in their life, they always have God. There's less worry and stress because they feel better about the big picture."

Bill continued, "Maybe God answers prayers about health by keeping you happy through prayer. There's a connection between mental and physical health, so if praying keeps you relaxed, you'll feel better overall."

O Lord, let Your ear be attentive to the prayer of Your servant, and to the prayer of Your servants who delight in revering Your name. (Nehemiah 1:11)

Jesus, teach me to pray as You did.

Responsibility Enriches You

"God gives the nuts, but He does not crack them," says an old German proverb. In short, it means that the Lord wishes each of us to work with Him in solving problems, small and large.

By accepting this responsibility, you will:

- Learn not only to think for yourself, but also how to put your original ideas to work.

- Discover hidden talent that you never realized you possessed.

- Become self-reliant when your own experiences prove that your contribution is needed.

- Show more daring for good once you discover ways and means, on your own initiative, to solve problems affecting everybody.

- Develop your imagination and enterprise each time you strive to be a "self-starter."

- Enjoy the sense of personal fulfillment that God promises to those who, while depending on Him, put to good use the reasonable independence which He expects each of us to show.

Ask, and it will be given you...knock, and the door will be opened for you. (Matthew 7:7)

Help me, Divine Master, to face my responsibilities.

When It's Worth Getting Fired

When Jim Caviezel first arrived in Hollywood to pursue an acting career, he once took a job as a waiter, helping to cater a party at a famous producer's house. The caterer told the wait staff that if he saw any of them engaging in conversation with the celebrity guests, they would be fired on the spot.

Caviezel did his job as told. But then, he saw his favorite actor, Jimmy Stewart, who he admired not just for his on-screen work, but also his military service. Caviezel decided he was willing to get fired for talking to Stewart, so he approached him. The young actor was humbled by how friendly, gracious, and forthcoming the veteran was.

Sure enough, the caterer saw this and signaled that he should leave. Caviezel thanked Stewart for talking to him, and the elder man responded, "Young man, you go make good movies." Caviezel stayed in touch with Stewart until his death, and still cherishes the time they spent together. In 2015, Caviezel accepted the Harvey Award from the James Stewart Museum Foundation for the integrity he's brought to his life and work.

He stores up sound wisdom for the upright. (Proverbs 2:7)

Guide me toward risks worth taking, Holy Spirit.

Joy is a Choice

Former Director of The Christophers Father John Catoir has long been focused on being a "messenger of joy," which is also the name of his website. He was influenced by his study of the gospels as well as Pope John Paul II's emphasis on joy as an integral part of Christian living.

During an interview on "Christopher Closeup," he explained, "Jesus said, 'Be not afraid.' And those words are repeated in the Bible 365 times from the beginning to the end... The point was to trust the Lord, trust in His love. We have so much going for us, God has given us so many gifts. What can you help do but be joyful and be grateful? And it changes your life, it takes you out of the blues!"

Ultimately, Father Catoir has learned that joy is a choice, so he chooses to approach life that way: "I'm 84. I've had three knee replacements, I don't walk too well. And from the neck up, I'm fantastic every other day! (laughs) I have a heart condition, but I'm happy as a clam! I can't tell you I'm ready to go, but I'm gonna do as much good as I can until I am taken."

In Your presence there is fullness of joy. (Psalm 16:11)

Divine Messiah, help me to choose joy today.

The Shirt Off His Back

Did you ever hear the one about the New Yorker who'd give you the shirt off his back? No? Then consider the case of Joey Resto—because he actually did that one day last year. And on the subway, no less.

It seems that Resto, a paralegal who comes from Brooklyn, was riding the A train in Washington Heights when he saw a shirtless man sitting across from him, looking as if he might have been in a fight. He must have been cold, Resto reasoned, because it was wintertime.

Resto then did something that the rest of us wished we had the courage to do: he literally gave the man the shirt off his back.

"He was warm for the first time in I don't know how long," Resto told New York *Daily News* transit reporter Dan Rivoli. "He just curled up in a corner and went to sleep."

Resto tried to talk the man into going for a hot meal with him, but to no avail. He did record the encounter on video, however, and posted it on Facebook, where it received 300,000 "Likes" from people who appreciated his spirit of generosity.

Whoever has two coats must share with anyone who has none. (Luke 3:11)

Generous God, may I always act on the impulse to give.

The Good Thief

For six months, a four-foot statue of Jesus stood in front of the Angels & Company gift shop in Monroe, Connecticut. As reported by New York's *Daily News,* "The faded, chipped Jesus figure [was] a gift from a store patron who moved and couldn't take it with him."

Then, one day, the statue was gone. The store's co-owner, Midge Saglimbene, called the police, who didn't have any immediate luck finding the thief. A few days later—November 1st, or All Saints Day, to be exact—Saglimbene received a call from a friend exclaiming, "Jesus is back!"

The friend had been driving by the shop when she discovered that the statue had been returned. And not only returned, but improved. Reporter Meg Wagner wrote, "[Jesus's] faded orange shawl was repainted a bright scarlet, and his chipped hair and beard were also retouched with new paint."

Saglimbene doesn't know who took the statue, but she now refers to the person as "the good thief."

Thieves must give up stealing; rather let them labor and work honestly with their own hands. (Ephesians 4:28)

Help me improve the world's vision of You, Jesus.

Winning the Sainthood Lottery

When Powerball fever swept the nation in 2016, *CBS News* reported that people had a higher chance of "achieving sainthood" than winning the big lottery. It's likely *CBS* meant being canonized a saint. But sainthood in general is more achievable because it's not a game of luck; there's choice involved, along with a good helping of God's grace.

It's important to remember that people who've died and made it to heaven are considered saints. All of them, not just the ones who have official feast days. That means your mom, dad, grandma or grandpa could be a saint right now and praying for you to join them some day.

Faith, action, and nurturing a relationship with God are needed to achieve this eternal goal. And if we keep our eyes open, the grace we need will be there to guide us, too. No canonized saint was ever perfect, and we'll never be perfect either. But when saints fall, they admit and atone for their mistake, and move forward in the right direction. Surely, we can do the same.

You are citizens with the saints. (Ephesians 2:19)

Lord, I want to be in that number when the saints go marching in.

Emmaus Ministry for Grieving Parents

After their 26-year-old son Paul committed suicide for no apparent reason, Diane and Charlie Monaghan felt devastated and overwhelmed with grief. Though they attended counseling and support groups, nothing helped—until they sought spiritual direction from a Franciscan sister.

Diane told *Catholic Digest's* Lori Hadacek Chaplin, "My spiritual director said over and over again: 'With death, life has changed, but it has not ended. Paul is very much still alive.' That was the only thing that brought my husband and I any kind of peace and comfort—focusing on the promise of eternal life and the fact that Paul is still very much with us."

To help others in similar situations, the Monaghans founded the Emmaus Ministry for Grieving Parents (www.emfgp.org), in association with the Franciscan Friars at Boston's St. Anthony Shrine. While the retreats are Catholic, Charlie said, "We have had Protestant and Jewish parents come, and all of them have told us that it was beneficial and beautiful."

Blessed are those who mourn, for they will be comforted. (Matthew 5:4)

May the promise of eternal life comfort the grieving, Lord.

The Prisoner in the Abbey

Heroic priests served as chaplains in the German armed forces during the World Wars, often dying martyrs' deaths. According to *Salute,* magazine of the Archdiocese of the Military Services, USA, one such chaplain was Blessed Rupert Mayer, a Jesuit priest, who was beatified by St. John Paul in 1997.

Father Mayer first volunteered during World War I, receiving the Iron Cross for bravery and losing his left leg in a grenade attack. At great peril, he distributed the sacraments to his men, reaching their side in the trenches and listening thoughtfully to their hopes and fears.

From Hitler's rise to power in 1933, Father Mayer repeatedly preached against the dictator, and was eventually imprisoned by the Nazis. Held in an abbey rather than a concentration camp—for fear of the publicity that would result—he died there in 1945 from the toll that prison life had taken on his weakened body. His feast day is observed on November 3.

Even though I walk through the darkest valley, I fear no evil; for You are with me. (Psalm 23:4)

Good Shepherd, give me knowledge of Your presence and the courage to share You with others.

Wiser at 90 Than at 80

Father John Clay has no plans to retire. Why should he? At 90, he's the St. Paul-Minneapolis Archdiocese's oldest pastor, true, but he feels great! And as long as he's got his Twitter ministry to send out his messages, he can focus on spiritual counseling and preparing Catholics to receive the sacraments.

Since 1975 Father Clay has been pastor of St. Stanislaus in St. Paul. He was the first non-Czech chosen for that post, and he readily admits he's still learning. When a fire damaged the Lutheran church nearby, he told Susan Klemond of *The Catholic Spirit*, he offered to have them move in. "We've got a lot to learn from each other," he said.

"I'm not the same as I was in 1975," he added. "What I've finally come to understand is that I have learned more about what it means to be a Christian since I was 80 than in the first 80 years of my life."

Who is wise and understanding among you? Show by your good life that your works are done with gentleness born of wisdom. (James 3:13)

May I always be open to new life lessons, Redeemer.

A Second Chance at Abi's Cafe

Cesia Abigail Baires runs the Salvadoran restaurant Abi's Cafe in Minneapolis, where homeless people often come in to ask for money. One day, a man named Marcus entered with a similar request.

Baires told *ABC News,* "There are a lot of people who walk in, there are a lot of drugs and crime in this area. If they ask me for money, I offer food. I told him nothing is given to me for free, just to see what his reaction was going to be. Some people might take that as an offense."

Instead, Marcus shared his own story, explaining that nobody wanted to hire him because he has a record of committing felonies. He also said that some restaurants won't even let someone who looks homeless into the building.

Baires found that kind of treatment "unacceptable," so she offered Marcus work as a dishwasher. He happily accepted and has been doing a good job. Baires was also impressed by his character. When she gave him food that first day, he gave half of it away to another homeless person that he knew was hungry.

Give some of your food to the hungry. (Tobit 4:16)

Lead repentant sinners to the second chances they so desperately need, Lord.

'A Special Breed of Warrior'

President Obama called him "a special breed of warrior" the day he awarded the Congressional Medal of Honor to Edward C. Byers last year, and that pretty much sums up the Navy SEAL's courageous character. Byers said later that he plans to "continue doing my job in the Navy."

As Mark Mazzetti and Gardiner Harris told the story in *The New York Times,* Byers rushed into an enemy compound even after another SEAL was shot in the head. He wrestled with a Taliban gunman and subsequently dived on top of Dr. Dilip Joseph, an American being held hostage, to protect him from gunfire. Then, when the operation was over, a helicopter spirited Byers and Dr. Joseph to safety.

"Today's ceremony is truly unique," the president said as he presented the award. "It's a rare opportunity for the American people to get a glimpse of a special breed of warrior that so often serves in the shadows."

I have fought the good fight; I have finished the race; I have kept the faith. (2 Timothy 4:7)

May I be faithful and courageous in the battles You give me to fight, Father.

A Lesson from Honest Abe

Abraham Lincoln's first paycheck as President saved taxpayers $273.97. In April 1861, Lincoln was asked to sign a letter requesting his salary "as President of the United States" be sent to him on the "first of each month."

With his own pen, Lincoln crossed out the word "first" and substituted "fifth." Since he had been inaugurated on March 4, 1861, he felt his annual salary of $25,000 should start the next day, March 5th.

This pen-scratch speaks volumes. It is convincing proof of how conscientious Lincoln was in small matters as well as large ones. By refusing to accept pay for the first four days of March, on the grounds that he was not entitled to it, "Honest Abe" set an example for us all.

Help promote the conviction that honesty in government and in every other place can start with each one of us. God will bless your efforts and you will render a much-needed service.

Because the Lord loved Israel forever, He has made you king to execute justice and righteousness. (1 Kings 10:9)

Help me to be scrupulously honest, O Holy Spirit, with everything that does not belong to me.

Called To Be a Family

Karen Mott puts her heart into her job as a nurse at the MetroWest Cancer Center in Framingham, Massachusetts. Never was that more true than in 2011, when she met Patricia McNulty, a single mother battling an aggressive—and eventually, fatal—cancer. McNulty's nine-year-old son Stephen was the light of her life, and she worried what would happen to him when she passed on, since his father was disabled and couldn't care for him.

Mott, a mother of three, had met Stephen and thought he was unusually intelligent and kind for his age. Her husband Michael, who works as the hospice chaplain at MetroWest, felt the same way. As Mott recalled in *Reader's Digest,* they both believed that God was calling them to welcome Stephen into their family—and that's what they did.

They supported him through the heartache of his mother's death and gave him the love he needed to move forward. Recently, Stephen had to write a poem about "Home" for school. He ended it with words about his new life with the Motts: "Home is feeling cared for, loved, and protected."

In You the orphan finds mercy. (Hosea 14:3)

Inspire families to be open to new life through adoption or foster care, Father.

Kindness Hits the Right Notes

Growing up in Poland, Joseph Feingold played the violin every day, displaying a love and talent for the instrument. Then, the Nazis came, and his family was sent to a concentration camp. Joseph survived, but others did not. He felt the loss.

In 1947, Feingold spotted a beautiful violin at a flea market in Germany. The seller gave it to him for a carton of cigarettes. Playing the instrument revived Feingold's spirit, and it became his companion for the next 70 years.

Now a New Yorker, the 91-year-old decided to pass his violin on to someone in whose hands it could continue making beautiful music. *WNYC* reported that he donated it to *WQXR's* Instrument Drive. They gave it to Brianna, a student at The Bronx Global Learning Institute for Girls who, her teachers say, has a "unique ability to show her emotion through her violin."

When the 12-year-old met Feingold, they bonded over their love of music. She told filmmaker Kahane Cooperman, who made a documentary about this story, "Everyone has those days when it's dark for them, but most people find their light. And my light was playing the violin."

Praise Him with strings and pipe! (Psalm 150:4)

May I extend my hand to the next generation, Father.

God's Firefighter

When St. Joseph's Seminary of the New York Archdiocese turned loose its class of newly-ordained priests last spring, it had an honest-to-goodness New York City firefighter—its first—among them.

He is Father Thomas Colucci, 60, and his wishes are simple: "I want to serve the people of God," he says. He'll get his initial crack at that in his first assignment, St. Mary's in Fishkill. He's looking forward to it. "I just love the people in New York," he said. "There's nothing like our city."

Father Colucci had already begun checking out the priesthood as a career after he left the fire department in the aftermath of an explosion, which led to his early retirement. After two surgeries, he joined the Benedictines, then entered the seminary system.

Following an assignment at the annual Fire Department Memorial Mass at St. Patrick's Cathedral, he'll have a full dose of parish life, and that's fine by him. "I'm very, very happy," he said. "The Lord's blessed me."

Immediately they left their nets and followed Him. (Mark 1:18)

Son of God, may I listen for and follow Your call.

Tough As They Come, Part One

On April 10, 2012—four days before his 25th birthday—U.S. Army Staff Sergeant Travis Mills was on his third tour in Afghanistan when an IED explosion ripped off his right arm and right leg. Over the next few days, he lost his left arm and leg as well, making him one of only five quadruple amputees from the wars in Iraq and Afghanistan to survive these injuries.

During an interview on "Christopher Closeup" about his Christopher Award-winning memoir "Tough As They Come," Mills said that next to the excruciating pain he endured for some time, he worried about what his wife Kelsey and baby daughter Chloe would think of his new condition. He feared the six-month-old would see him as a "monster."

Kelsey, however, loved him through it all and vowed to stay by his side. And despite Mills being laid up in the hospital connected to tubes and machines, Chloe, he says, "just saw me as regular old Dad." That visit, he admits, brought tears to his eyes. But Mills had another challenge to deal with: his anger at God. That part of the story tomorrow.

Carry me out of the battle, for I am wounded. (1 Kings 22:34)

Bring wounded soldiers the support they need, Savior.

Tough As They Come, Part Two

It's not surprising that after losing both arms and both legs to an IED explosion in Afghanistan, U.S. Army Staff Sergeant Travis Mills felt let down by God. After all, he lived life the right way, so why would God punish him, he wondered.

Then, his sister-in-law brought him a plaque with a quote from the book of Joshua: "Be strong and courageous. Do not be afraid. Do not be discouraged for the Lord your God will be with you wherever you go."

Mills asked her to get rid of it, but she refused. Eventually, he came to the realization "that it's not fair to only believe when things are going my way...I'm fortunate enough to still be alive. I had my family, I had the ability to do things."

Now, with assistance from prosthetic arms and legs, Mills runs a foundation to help other wounded veterans. He's also able to drive and make breakfast for his wife and daughter. He doesn't want any pity ("I just had one bad day at work," he says), but hopes to be a blessing and inspiration to others.

The testing of your faith produces endurance. (James 1:3)

Lord, I believe; help my unbelief.

Bringing Love to a Warzone

The Aurora Prize for Awakening Humanity was created in 2016 to honor people who have risked and sacrificed a great deal in order to "preserve human life in the face of adversity," reported *CNN*. And the first winner sure fits the bill.

Burundi's 12-year civil war between Hutus and Tutsis began in 1993, resulting in 300,000 casualties. After Marguerite Barankitse, a Tutsi, witnessed the murder of 72 of her Hutu neighbors, she resolved to be a force for peace.

CNN stated, "[She started] a mission at the Catholic diocese where she worked. Caring for children and refugees, she created an environment where young Hutus and Tutsis alike could seek refuge." Her efforts saved 30,000 children.

Actor George Clooney presented Barankitse with the one million dollar Aurora Prize, which she will donate to the support of orphans and refugees. She said, "When you have compassion, dignity and love, then nothing can scare you, nothing can stop you. No one can stop love—not armies, not hate, not persecution, not famine, nothing."

Religion that is pure...before God...is this: care for orphans and widows in their distress. (James 1:27)

Guide those who heal the wounds of war, Prince of Peace.

You Can Help Fight Loneliness

Loneliness is a problem for many in our society, especially the elderly. A study conducted by the Universities of California and Chicago suggests it might cause health issues as well.

As reported by Jessica and Tim Lahey in *The Atlantic,* researchers discovered that genes that fight viral infections are lower in socially isolated seniors. In addition, genes that cause inflammation and contribute to disease are higher.

What can be done? The Laheys highlight a program in Lyme, New Hampshire, called Veggie Cares, which "distributes local food to people living alone...Volunteers also deliver companionship. Visits...may involve a shared cup of tea, an offer to replace burned-out light bulbs, or a chance to check in on sick or elderly neighbors."

Loneliness isn't always an obvious problem, but it's one we can all help fight. Reach out to those around you who may need nothing more than a friendly conversation to give their immune systems a boost.

Turn to me and be gracious to me, for I am lonely and afflicted. (Psalm 25:16)

Creator, may we never undervalue the gift of our presence.

'The Right Officer at the Right Time'

When five-year-old David Samiel Jr. of Garfield, New Jersey, started choking on a quarter one day last year, his grandfather panicked as he called 911. "We were frantic," said the grandfather, David Samiel Sr.

Little did he know that Police Officer Francisco Sanchez was on patrol, only two blocks away. Fortunately, Sanchez was not only a cop, but also an emergency medical technician. By the grandfather's estimation, he was at the house within 20 seconds.

By that time, little David's eyes were rolling and he could barely breathe. Officer Sanchez wasted no time. He calmed the boy down, put him over his knee and struck him on his back four times—and out jumped the quarter. "Before you knew it, we heard the coin on the floor," the grandfather exclaimed. "Seconds after the officer helped him, he was 100 percent."

The next day, David, his father and grandfather visited the station house in person to say "Thank you" and to present Sanchez with a gift basket. Stefanie Dazio of *The Record* reported that Sanchez was "the right officer at the right time."

He said, "Young man, I say to you, rise!" (Luke 7:14)

Thank you, Lord Jesus, for quick-thinking heroes.

How a Letter Helped the Disabled

Despite some physical limitations from Cerebral Palsy, Matthew Walzer is a self-sufficient teenager except for one thing: he's not able to tie his shoelaces because he only "has flexibility in one hand," reported Nike.com. As a fan of Nike shoes, he wrote the company a letter explaining his problem and wondering if they might come up with a solution.

Walzer's letter wound up in the hands of Tobie Hatfield, who had been working on similar problems for disabled athletes involved with the Paralympics and Special Olympics. He contacted Walzer, and the two began collaborating.

In 2015, Nike FLYEASE was born. Modeled on the shoes of LeBron James (Walzer's favorite basketball player), they use "a wrap-around zipper" that allows you to easily slide your foot in and out, while also locking it down without needing laces.

Walzer is now attending Florida Gulf Coast University, where he wears his special shoes every day. He is grateful that Nike helped make life better for him and the many others who struggle with physical challenges.

He has filled him with divine spirit...to devise artistic designs. (Exodus 35:31-32)

Enhance my creative problem-solving skills, Creator.

Everybody's Doing It

Some years ago, a school superintendent in Arkansas noticed that a junior high school girl was wearing one red sock and one blue sock. He asked her if this had some special meaning.

The teenager explained that she was wearing different socks because she was an individualist. She said, "I have a right to be different if I want to—besides, all the kids are doing it."

Fads in clothing have long been a way for teenagers to assert their independence from parents and gain acceptance by peers. Conforming to peer pressure in the way they dress is usually harmless. But teens are often pressured to do dangerous things such as drinking or using drugs.

Parents can help teens resist harmful peer pressure by building up their confidence and teaching them what individuality really is.

[Clothe] yourselves with the new self, which is being renewed in knowledge according to the image of its Creator. (Colossians 3:10)

Jesus, inspire teens to follow Your ways, not dangerous fads.

Where Windshield Wipers Come From

The next time you're driving in the rain, don't forget to thank Mary Anderson. You see, she's the reason your car has windshield wipers. The website A Mighty Girl shared Anderson's story last year:

"Anderson was already a real estate developer and rancher when she visited New York City in 1902 and rode on a trolley car where the driver had to open the panes of the front window in order to see through falling sleet. As soon as she returned home to Alabama, she set to work conceiving a solution.

"Her device used a lever inside the vehicle to control a rubber blade on the windshield; similar devices had been made earlier, but Anderson's was the first effective model. Amazingly, car manufacturers initially didn't see the value in her invention.

"However, in 1922, Cadillac became the first car manufacturer to include a windshield wiper on all its vehicles, and after Anderson's patent expired, they quickly became standard equipment."

He has filled him with...skill, intelligence, and knowledge in every kind of craft. (Exodus 35:31)

Divine Wisdom, help me to be a problem-solver.

Buying Underwear, Supporting Adoption

Debra Steigerwaldt Waller felt blessed to be adopted as a child, so as an adult, she knew she wanted to do something to promote that cause herself. The fact that she was adopted by the family that owns the Wisconsin-based underwear company Jockey International has made it easier to give back.

As reported by the *Milwaukee Journal Sentinel,* Waller became chairman and CEO of Jockey in 2001, and eventually decided to create a charitable arm of the company, called Jockey Being Family. They work with two agencies to provide post-adoption support for families—and Jockey's own company cafeteria houses shelves filled with blankets, games, and other items for children who will be placed with families.

Jockey has donated over one million dollars to adoption causes, and they give their U.S. employees who adopt a child special benefits. "I know the Lord put me here for a reason," Waller says. "In my mind, every kid should have a home."

Let the little children come to Me...It is to such as these that the kingdom of heaven belongs. (Matthew 19:14)

Open the hearts of modern families to adoption, Creator.

Tips for a Stress-Free Thanksgiving

Thanksgiving is a wonderful time for gathering with family and friends, but it can also be stressful for those who have long distances to travel or relatives with whom they don't get along. Jennifer Sawyer, writing for the website Busted Halo, feels their pain and offers tips for a stress-free Thanksgiving:

- **Keep gratitude at the forefront.** "Begin dinner with a prayer, and encourage each member of your family to share what he or she is most grateful for this year."

- **Let annoyances slide.** "Is well-meaning Aunt Sally asking yet again why you're not married? Grandpa Joe letting everyone else know why their specific political views will destroy the world? Today is the day to take a deep breath and let it slide. If you find yourself feeling resentful, pause and say a prayer instead. And if you're looking for a tension-free conversation starter, turn on the Thanksgiving Day parade."

- **Help and laugh.** Offer to help the host or hostess set the table or clean up after the meal. Play games that bring out everyone's silly side. Thanksgiving is, after all, a fun and happy occasion.

Let there be thanksgiving. (Ephesians 5:4)

May I choose gratitude over stress as I gather with loved ones, Prince of Peace.

The Gospel of Happiness

"The happiness quotient is higher among people who *practice* religious faith, not just *have* religious faith."

That's what Dr. Christopher Kaczor discovered when he was researching his book "The Gospel of Happiness." In other words, the many Americans who attend religious services every week are more likely to be happy.

Kaczor relates this to his own experience of going to Mass. During a "Christopher Closeup" interview, he said, "The very last words of the Mass are 'Thanks be to God.' Every Mass is a chance to offer thanksgiving.

"One of the interesting things I learned is that the fewest number of people commit suicide on Thanksgiving Day because that's when people turn their minds and hearts to what they have and what they're grateful for, rather than just focusing on what they don't have. As Catholics, we're fortunate because we have Thanksgiving not just once a year, but at every single Mass because the Eucharist is a Greek term for 'thanksgiving.'"

Let us come into His presence with thanksgiving. (Psalm 95:2)

Help me to choose an attitude of gratitude, Holy Spirit.

Start a Gratitude List

"To-do" lists are pretty common but what about a "gratitude list"? As Arthur C. Brooks wrote in *The New York Times,* "For many people, gratitude is difficult, because life is difficult. Even beyond deprivation and depression, there are many ordinary circumstances in which gratitude doesn't come easily."

We can still act grateful in spite of how we're really feeling, says Brooks. Acting "as if" we feel gratitude might actually change our mood. "Choosing to focus on good things makes you feel better than focusing on bad things."

Most of us appreciate the value of good health, supportive families and friends, and sufficient resources. But there are other treasures to cherish: holding hands with a loved one, seeing sunrises and sunsets, listening to little children giggle, enjoying that funny email or yet another cat video, mending fences with an old friend.

Because there is probably a link between being grateful and feeling good, a gratitude list seems like a fine idea.

**Our God, we give thanks to You.
(1 Chronicles 29:13)**

May we always be grateful for Your gifts, Jesus.

The Pizza Delivery Man's Surprising Tip

It was Sunday morning in Mentor, Ohio, and Gionino's Pizzeria wasn't even officially open yet. But 22-year-old delivery man Jeff Louis came in early because the congregation at Life Point Church had ordered several pizzas.

Since it was Thanksgiving week, Pastor Ken Wright decided to surprise Louis with a $100 tip in front of the whole congregation. Then, the random act of kindness grew in an unexpected way. All the church members started coming up to give Louis extra tip money. When it was all over, the surprised and humbled pizza delivery man had collected $700.

Louis took to Youtube to tell the world about the kindness of these strangers. He also revealed an addiction issue they hadn't known about: "I've been having such a hard time lately, just struggling to stay clean and I'm just trying to get my life back...It really truly amazes me that people who don't even know me just wanted to help me out that much."

Pastor Wright was surprised, too, and credited God with helping Louis when he needed it most. He said, "We can change the world one life at a time."

Kindness is like a garden of blessings. (Sirach 40:17)

May I be generous in sharing blessings, Lord.

Kindness and the Road to Sainthood

Kindness comes from the Old English word for family. It is *within* the family that we learn kindness, help for those in need, and a thoughtful attitude.

And it is *from* the family that we carry kindness—a thoughtful attitude and a desire to help the needy through our jobs, our community, our fellow worshipers.

Not that kindness is easy. It isn't always simple for either the giver or the receiver, and it can even become a burden. But it is always humane and humanizing.

Jesus taught the need for kindness when He told the parable of the Good Samaritan and his praiseworthy deed of kindness on that desolate desert road down to Jericho from Jerusalem. As Jan van Ruysbroeck, a medieval Rhenish mystic, wrote, "Be kind, be kind, be kind, and you will soon be saints."

Pleasant words are like a honeycomb, sweetness to the soul and health to the body. (Proverbs 16:24)

Help me be kind to myself, and may my speech and actions towards others be gracious, strong yet gentle Jesus.

A Unique Retirement Trip

In 2006, a 71-year-old man from the Midwest took a retirement trip to Tanzania and answered a plea for help. Ten years later, this same man, Jim Vanderheyden of Brooklyn Park, Minnesota, finds himself heading a nonprofit called the Tanzania Life Project (TLP). TLP provides water to thousands of Tanzanians, answering as directly as possible the biblical injunction to give drink to the thirsty.

Jim and his wife, Katie, have often volunteered their services during 60-plus years of marriage, and TLP took advantage of his employment history as an engineer with Honeywell. He rolled up his sleeves and went to work, and there's no end in sight.

Now, Vanderheyden makes several trips to Tanzania in a year and heads a list of donors that provide millions of dollars that go directly to villages in the African nation's back country.

"When you go over there, you see that they have nothing," said Katie. "Everyone should have clean water."

I give water in the wilderness, rivers in the desert, to give drink to My chosen people. (Isaiah 43:20)

Guide me to see where Your people are thirsting, Lord, and help me bring them what they need.

Lead More Than a Harmless Life

A critic once summed up a movie as follows: "Not remarkable, but pleasant and no harm done." That terse judgment could also serve as an epitaph for many people who contentedly live a mediocre life. It's easy to slip into a passive or negative way of living. But those who smugly boast, "I've never done any harm to anyone," and think that's the peak of achievement really miss the big reason for living.

Nowhere in the Gospels does our Lord advise us to take it easy. Jesus repeatedly stresses that we should use our talent and not bury it by leading lives that are nothing better than harmless.

He emphasizes that our very salvation depends on the positive good we do for others with the gifts He has entrusted to us. Do good, He commands. Avoiding evil is not enough. Love your neighbor, He insists. That means far more than just tolerating or refraining from hurting others.

Let your light shine before others, so that they may see your good works and give glory to your Father in heaven. (Matthew 5:16)

Deepen in me, O Lord, a yearning to fill my life with good deeds, not merely to avoid harm.

Simple Meal Changes a Life

"Excuse me, lady. Do you have any spare change? I'm hungry." Those were the first words that 11-year-old Maurice Mazyck spoke to Laura Schroff as she passed him on a New York City street back in 1986.

Schroff initially said, "No," but then she reconsidered because the words "I'm hungry" stuck with her. She bought Maurice lunch, and that led to a lifelong friendship between the advertising executive and the boy who lived in a shelter hotel.

During an interview about her Christopher Award-winning children's book "An Invisible Thread Christmas Story," Schroff revealed that since she didn't have any children herself, Maurice was like an answer to a prayer. And as he was exposed to Schroff's extended family—especially for big, fun meals around the dining room table—he came to see new possibilities for his own future.

Sure enough, Maurice's home today has a dining room. He's been married for over 20 years, has seven beautiful children, and works in the construction industry.

I would give my food to the hungry. (Tobit 1:17)

Show me how I can feed hungry bodies and souls, Father.

A Heavenly Joke

The November 2015 issue of *Reader's Digest* included the favorite jokes of several celebrities. Comedian Gilbert Gottfried offered this riddle: "Why did the horses get a divorce? They didn't have a stable relationship."

Actor Oscar Nuñez, who played Oscar Martinez on the TV series "The Office," shared this story: "In heaven, there were two huge signs. The first read, *Men Who Did What Their Wives Told Them to Do.* The line of men under this sign stretched as far as the eye could see.

"The second sign stated, *Men Who Did What They Wanted to Do.* Only one man stood under that sign. Intrigued, St. Peter said to the lone man, 'No one has ever stood under this sign. Tell me about yourself.'

"The man shrugged and said, 'Not much to say; my wife told me to stand here.'"

All the days of the poor are hard, but a cheerful heart has a continual feast. (Proverbs 15:15)

Life is full of challenges, Lord, so let me bolster my spirits by finding something to laugh about every day.

Comedian and Priest Join Forces for Good

Jay Leno is using retirement from "The Tonight Show" to do some good—and he teamed up with Father Jim Sichko, a priest at St. Mark Catholic Church in Richmond, Kentucky, to get it done.

In November 2015, police officer Daniel Ellis was shot and killed while investigating the robbery of a kindergarten teacher at St. Mark's school. He left behind a wife, Katie, and three-year-old son, Luke. Determined to help the family because Officer Ellis's murder hit close to home, Father Sichko gifted Katie and Luke with a trip to Disney World. He also arranged for Leno to come do a fundraiser that would benefit the family.

As reported by *WKYT-TV,* Leno himself donated $10,000 to support Luke's college fund. He said, "Everybody thinks the world is such a terrible place, but there are more good people than there are bad people...This police officer that was killed in the line of duty, he was a good man."

Katie expressed thanks for all the support she is receiving and said, "I feel like the community is really healing with me."

O Lord, heal me. (Psalm 6:2)

Bring healing to those who've lost loved ones, Savior.

Put Others First, Find Happiness

Most of us want to be happy. We seek fulfillment, but all too often we do not seem to find it. In fact, there is a simple way. It comes by putting the focus on others.

Start by asking yourself, "What good can I do for someone today?" Consider all the people around you, at home, on the job, in your neighborhood. Then do something. It doesn't have to be a big favor, it can be as simple as a compliment on a job well done.

Then do something harder: be nice to a person you dislike or who dislikes you. It might be tough to do even a little thing, but a friendly gesture can help both of you.

Finally, single out a person you usually ignore and say or do something to make them feel special.

If you want to be happy yourself, be kind to others. Maintain constant love for one another, for love covers a multitude of sins. (1 Peter 4:8)

Spirit of the living God, how can I be kind today?

A Hug to Save a Life

An off-duty New York police officer out Christmas shopping with his family discovered a new way to avert a suicide: an old-fashioned hug.

Officer Christian Campoverde was at the Queens Center mall with his wife and children when a man dashed past them, mumbling something about taking his life. At his family's urging, Campoverde sprang into action.

The man had his leg over the third floor balcony railing and was ready to jump when the officer caught up to him. He remembered his team training on crisis intervention and said, "My name is Chris. I don't know what you're going through, but I know it must be pretty bad—but trust me, it's not worth it. Is it okay if I give you a hug? Do you want a hug?"

Campoverde told Dana Sauchelli of the *New York Post* that he then embraced the man, who promptly burst into tears. "He cried hard for a good four to five minutes," the cop said. Once the man had composed himself, EMS took him in for evaluation.

He took her by the hand and said..."Little girl, get up." And immediately, the girl got up. (Mark 5:41-42)

Holy Physician, may I always be willing to reach out a hand to those in need.

The Strong Hand of Hope

Whenever you feel like you need to lean on God for strength and guidance, consider saying this prayer from the Society of the Little Flower:

"It is so good to hold Your hand and walk with You, Holy God of the Journey. Yours is the strong hand of hope. You promise new and renewed life for Your people. You have gardener's hands. Through Your coming and work, the dried-up landscape of our souls will be watered and blossom again in fruitful life. Your digging and embracing hands work wonders.

"Lord Jesus, John announced Your coming like the new Elijah. Help us to see You coming in our world. Help us to grasp Your hand as You walk with us in our lives, Emmanuel. May Your hand heal violence and bring inner peace which enables us to hear and listen to You, whispering and shouting in our world, in our history! I love Your strong grip and firm handshake, Holy God!!! Your outstretched hand fills the journey with hope."

In Your steadfast love You led the people whom You redeemed; You guided them by Your strength to Your holy abode. (Exodus 15:13)

Guide me this day toward a future with hope, Savior.

No Such Thing as a Small Act of Love

During Advent 2015, Simcha Fisher read a story in the *Washington Post* about Roots of Empathy, a Washington, D.C. program "which has teachers in poor, tough neighborhoods welcoming babies into their classrooms." Each student greets the baby, then they observe the child in different situations, building empathy for what he or she is feeling.

The results are promising, having brought about "more peace, more respect, and better learning" in the classroom, Fisher writes on the website Aleteia. And she relates this to how all of us should be transformed by the birth of Jesus:

"The older I get, the more I realize that the whole point of the Incarnation is that the divine and the mundane are now inextricably linked. There cannot be a meaningless act of service, because of the incomprehensibly great service God has performed for us. There is no longer any such thing as a small act of love, since God, who is love, became small and asked us to care for Him. There is literally nothing greater, more meaningful, or more transcendent we can do than to care for each other for His sake. All acts of love are great."

Love your neighbor as yourself. (Matthew 19:19)

May my acts of service reflect Your love, Messiah.

A Navy Pilot's Sacrifice

On December 4, 1959, a gallant jet fighter pilot stayed at the controls of his disabled plane till it crashed in San Diego, California, in order to prevent it from hitting a school with 1,000 children.

Just before he met his death, this heroic twenty-one-year-old Navy flier, Ensign Albert Hickman, of Sioux City, Iowa, frantically waved at the children of Hawthorne Elementary School who were eating lunch in the school playground, in a desperate effort to warn them to run.

Only God knows what thoughts raced through the mind of the brave young pilot during the last minute or so of his life. The desire for self-preservation must have been compelling. But his love for others was far more powerful.

Behind this noble self-sacrifice, Ensign Hickman must have had long and deep convictions. Seldom does one rise to heights of "greater love" unless it has been always a dominant factor in his life.

No one has greater love than this, to lay down one's life for one's friends. (John 15:13)

Let me fill my heart with love for others, Divine Savior.

A God Hater's Transformation

After his "devoutly Catholic" father died of brain cancer, Roy Nirschel abandoned his own faith. In a letter to *Catholic Digest,* he revealed that he didn't become an atheist, but rather a "God hater. I was angry that God allowed a man who lived the gospel to succumb to such a sudden and debilitating death."

Nirschel pursued a career as an educator, which brought him plenty of money and accolades. But it also resulted in an over-inflated ego, which led to the end of his marriage—and soon, all the prestige and fame he valued so much. "For me, effectively, my life was over," he said.

After moving to New York City, he one day passed the Church of St. Francis of Assisi and decided to go in. He found himself in the lower church chapel surrounded by tourists, immigrants, and homeless people—"the lost souls of the city." Nirschel cried because he realized he was a lost soul as well.

That experience reawakened his faith. With help from a priest, he returned to the Church and is now trying "to live the gospel in my daily life," just like his beloved father used to do.

Call to Me and I will answer you. (Jeremiah 33:3)

Transform hatred to humility and love for You, Jesus.

A Caring Santa

In 2015, the photo of a mall Santa playing on the floor with six-year-old Brayden Deely, who has autism, went viral. It was a picture that Brayden's mother Erin never thought would happen.

She told People.com, "I thought we would never get those holiday pictures with him because it's something he can't handle—the noise, and the pressure."

When Autism Speaks' Caring Santa program held a private event at the Deelys' local mall in Charlotte, North Carolina, they decided to give it a try, hoping the atmosphere would be more laid back. Santa could see that Brayden was a little apprehensive about approaching him, so Father Christmas placed a musical snow globe on the floor, then moved away. Brayden crawled over to examine the toy—and soon after, so did Santa.

Erin said, "They didn't even talk to each other, really, they just bonded and played, and Brayden started to be really excited and started looking at him and smiling." She concluded, "I just want to hug this man. He's so wonderful!"

Whoever welcomes one such child in My name welcomes Me. (Mark 9:37)

Bring joy to families of special needs children, Jesus.

Finding Family in Friends

When Katrina moved to a new city in Wisconsin that kept her quite a distance from her family and friends, she set out to find a faith community that shared her values.

Through her church, she joined the "First Saturday Rosary Group," in which parishioners would meet for dinner, prayer, and fellowship in a different person's home every month. She also joined a folk dance group through an acquaintance at work. After the dance, the group would head to an ice cream shop "where we got to know each other on a deeper level," she says.

Finally, after being trained by her parish priest, Katrina began bringing the Eucharist to five elderly parish members. They genuinely enjoyed the break from their loneliness and even said, "I love you," to her as they said their farewells.

Katrina concluded, "I believe God looks upon our hearts and sees our longing for community. Though friends do not replace our immediate families, they can become a source of great joy and teach us many things about serving others."

If we walk in the light as He himself is in the light, we have fellowship with one another. (1 John 1:7)

Inspire me to seek out new friendships, Holy Spirit.

A Greater Glory

Every teenager typically has one or more hobbies, such as reading, playing sports, etc. Daniel Wilkins, 13, participates in all these activities, but he also enjoys a unique and inspiring pastime—crafting his own rosary beads.

Wilkins's business began simply enough. He started selling homemade rosaries at his local church. All of the money Daniel made from selling these rosaries was immediately donated back to his parish of St. Francis de Sales in North Kingstown, Rhode Island, for both their building and charitable needs. Today, he enjoys a steady influx of business on his personally designed website, aptly named "A Greater Glory."

Five percent of all Wilkins's profits are donated to charity, and he even provides a special service where he repairs broken rosary beads for free. This practice originated as a courtesy to the elderly of the Legion of Mary nursing home, a place where Daniel often volunteers with his mother. "It's good to see him sharing his faith with other people," Wilkins's father, Jay, told *Rhode Island Catholic's* Laura Clem.

Like good stewards...serve one another with whatever gift each of you has received. (1 Peter 4:10)

Abba, may we use our talents for Your greater glory.

Dropping the Security Blanket

"A Charlie Brown Christmas" has been an annual TV favorite for over 50 years, owing largely to the story's inclusion of the religious element of the season. "Peanuts" creator Charles M. Schulz made sure to keep Christ in Christmas.

Though writer and musician Jason Soroski had seen the animated special many times, he noticed something new when re-watching it in 2015. Wherever he goes, the character Linus carries a security blanket to make himself feel safe. But when Linus is reciting the story of Jesus's birth from the Gospel of Luke, he drops the blanket when he quotes the line, "Fear not."

Writing for the website Crosswalk, Soroski observed, "It is pretty clear what Charles Schulz was saying...The birth of Jesus allows us to simply drop the false security we have been grasping so tightly, and learn to trust and cling to Him instead. In the midst of fear and insecurity, this simple cartoon image from 1965 continues to live on as an inspiration for us to seek true peace and true security in the one place it has always been and can always still be found."

Do not be afraid for see — I am bringing you good news of great joy. (Luke 2:10)

May Your presence be my greatest security blanket, Prince of Peace.

The Littlest Santa Claus

When Destinee McClung of Anchorage, Alaska, mentioned the topic of homelessness to her three-year-old son Patrick, he didn't know what the word meant. She explained that there were people in the city who had nowhere to live and nothing to eat. The boy started sobbing and even wanted to skip Christmas until she promised to help him collect donations for the homeless.

McClung told *ABC News* that she and Patrick set up "donation boxes around town, including at Patrick's preschool, his grandma's company, and a friend's chiropractic office. So far Patrick has collected 10 garbage bags full of cold weather gear, blankets, pillows, diapers, clothes, shoes and toys. Patrick even sold one of his toy trains...[to] buy more products to donate."

McClung sees her son as an inspiration: "Patrick has always been a very giving person and, for over a year, has wanted to be Santa when he grows up. He has done more for the homeless community in less than a month than I've done in my entire life."

**A generous person will be enriched.
(Proverbs 11:25)**

Help me see the less fortunate through the helpful eyes of a child, Prince of Peace.

A World Without Prayer?

Following the terror attacks in San Bernardino, California, in December 2015, many people took to social media to say they were praying for the victims and their families. This prompted many atheists to say that prayer was a waste of time. After all, it hasn't stopped bad things from happening in the world.

That naive view of prayer called to mind a 2012 "Christopher Closeup" interview with actor Jonathan Jackson who, when accepting an award for his role on "General Hospital," thanked the Monks of Mount Athos in Greece. Jackson explained that he had seen documentaries about the monks, who have been praying around the clock for 1,000 years.

He said, "These people [are] dedicating their lives to prayer. And not just praying for themselves, but praying for all of us. The thought crossed my mind: with all the destruction and insanity in this world, if their prayers weren't happening, what would this world be like? I felt personally like I wanted to thank them because I really believe that their prayers mean a lot."

Pray for one another. (James 5:16)

With fervent prayers, I ask You to heal this world, Creator.

Feeling Guilty About Happiness?

Juliann DosSantos always looks forward to the Christmas season and the joy and happiness it brings. But when a family member suffered a stroke in 2015, she struggled to find those feelings and questioned whether she wanted to celebrate the holidays at all.

Writing on her "Footprints on the Journey" blog for the *Catholic New York* website, she said, "Seeing how hard it is for this person to just get through makes me wonder if it's right for me to feel joyful or happy right now. I almost feel guilty when I feel that Christmas spirit slipping into my soul."

Then, DosSantos had an "epiphany...If I don't have any happiness or cheer inside myself, how can I bring anything like that to my relative who will need it more than ever this year? I realized that being joyful and happy isn't a selfish act, especially when you want to share that with people that you love."

There's no need to feel guilty about being joyful when others are suffering. Instead, use your joy to lift their spirits.

On the day I called, You answered me, You increased my strength of soul. (Psalm 138:3)

Lord, give me the strength to help bear the crosses of my loved ones and bring them Your joy and peace.

A Rabbi's Joke for the Pope

In the lead up to Pope Francis's first visit to the U.S. in 2015, the Pontifical Missions Society held a contest called "Joke with the Pope." Not only would the winner receive $10,000 to donate to one of three mission charities, he or she would be named "Honorary Comedic Advisor to the Pope."

Victory went to another man of faith: Rabbi (and stand-up comic) Bob Alper, who donated his prize to a facility for the homeless in Ethiopia. The 70-year-old East Dorset, Vermont resident joked to *PBS Newshour,* "I would always use jokes and funny stories in my sermons in front of my congregations, which would give me over 42 years of experience performing in front of a hostile audience."

Rabbi Alper believes that laughter has the power to bring people closer together and open our hearts to God. So what was his winning joke? "My wife and I have been married for over 46 years, and our lives are totally in sync. For example, at the same time I got a hearing aid, she stopped mumbling."

A cheerful heart is a good medicine.
(Proverbs 17:22)

Lord, You put opportunities for joy and laughter into my life. Show me a reason to smile every day.

Fantastic Friends Unite!

Marissa Hacker, 19, of Voorhees, New Jersey, is proud to be her brother's keeper—and then some. Her twin brother, Matthew, was diagnosed with autism at age two, and while he's good with numbers, he has trouble connecting with people his own age. "It was heartbreaking," Marissa told Louise Farr, who wrote their story in *Family Circle* magazine.

Marissa decided to do something about Matthew's loneliness. When she was 15, she rallied friends and classmates, and 20 people showed up for her first get-together for special-needs kids. "Matthew was so excited," she exclaimed. Marissa called the group Fantastic Friends.

Five years later, its monthly socials attract as many as 90 participants, and special-needs members range in age from 13 to 25. Their meetings include trips to special places, such as aquariums or a miniature golf park. Contributions take care of renting venue space, buying decorations and the like.

"When kids first come to the group they're quiet and shy," Marissa adds. "Then they just blossom."

Two are better than one; for if they fall, one will lift the other up. (Ecclesiastes 4:9-10)

Jesus, may I always be willing to lift others up.

What Ever Happened to Kindness?

In his book "Fresh Packet of Sower's Seeds," Father Brian Cavanaugh, T.O.R., recalled the Johnny Hart comic strip "B.C." in which the character Wiley asks, "What ever happened to kindness?" Hart then writes the following:

"Why do people go to the trouble to give other people some trouble? / Why do they burst someone's bubble, when they know it comes back to them double? / Why do we go to the effort to hurt someone we actually love? / Why can't we say something sweet 'stead of curt? A push only leads to a shove.

"Why can't we treat other folks with respect? With a smile or a kind word or two. / Treat them with honor, the way you'd expect they should act when they're dealing with you. / Why can't we overlook others' mistakes? We've all surely been there before. / Love and forgiveness is all that it takes, to boot Satan's butt out the door."

Father Cavanaugh concludes, "This Christmas season, give a gift that will last: 'Practice random kindness and senseless acts of beauty.'...The world could use a jolt such as this."

**Clothe yourselves with...kindness.
(Colossians 3:12)**

Guide me in practicing kindness today, Prince of Peace.

God, the Master Baker

Rita Buettner grew up with a father who loved baking cookies and made sure to involve his kids in the process, even if they made a mess or "ate three M&Ms for every one that made it onto a cookie."

When Buettner became a mom herself, she followed his example and learned a surprising lesson about baking with kids. As she wrote in the *Catholic Review*, newspaper of the Archdiocese of Baltimore, "Some flour lands in the bowl, but more lands on the table, chairs and floor...A child stirs so fervently that he sends the whole bowl spinning onto the floor."

Yet Buettner never remembers her father being anything but patient and enthusiastic. She then points out that God is likely the same way with her: "Day after day, He watches me stumble...Some days I put the wrong ingredients into the bowl... He knows I will fail many, many times, but He lets me try to do everything myself. And I can only learn and grow and be all He wants me to be if He lets me make my own decisions, under His watchful eye."

Deal with us in Your patience. (Daniel 3:42)

Thank You for Your patience, when I mess things up, Lord.

An Injured Seahawk Gives Back

Seattle Seahawks wide receiver Ricardo Lockette suffered a frightening injury in November 2015, during a game against the Dallas Cowboys. Patheos blogger Kate O'Hare wrote, "After taking a huge hit, [he] lay motionless on the ground."

The 29-year-old was rushed to a Dallas hospital, where surgeons operated on ligament damage in his neck. Thankfully, Lockette was released from the hospital five days later wearing a mandatory neck brace. He thanked his supporters via social media and gave credit to God for his recovery. He also decided that this was the perfect time to give back to the less fortunate.

When his ride passed through a section of town with a large homeless population, Lockette went to McDonald's, bought 100 cheeseburgers, and personally handed them out to those on the street. His father Earl told TMZ, "Through helping other people, he helped heal himself."

O'Hare concluded, "When you hear bad things about NFL players, remember, for every one of them, there are dozens like Lockette—tough, competitive guys who still have warm hearts and a strong faith."

He will feed His flock like a shepherd. (Isaiah 40:11)

Through helping others, may I find healing, Lord.

Christmas for Non-Believers

Families gather at Christmas time, but not everyone will be on the same page spiritually. Sister Theresa Aletheia Noble, a former atheist turned nun, knows that first-hand. She shared some thoughts in the *National Catholic Register* on being a positive influence on your loved ones during the holidays.

She notes, "When I was away from the Church...I was impressed by Christian friends and relatives who loved me for who I was and appreciated my gifts, my thoughts, and my time. When I felt like people were interacting with me as a means to an end, (i.e. just to convert me), I was turned off."

Also, "When I went home for Christmas as a fallen-away Catholic, I always knew that my parents would continue with the traditions of my childhood. We would carry Jesus to the manger on Christmas day, light Advent candles, and say prayers before opening gifts. My parents' piety was sometimes irritating to me. But all of these things built a foundation in me, a gut instinct that recognized that a Christmas without the spiritual can be glittering and glitzy, but ultimately empty of transcendent meaning."

**If we love one another, God lives in us.
(1 John 4:12)**

Teach me to love people as they are, Lord.

Three Ways to Inspire Children

Do you want to inspire your children to achieve great things? Here are three tips for parents:

- **Treat each child as an individual.** God gives slightly different talents and personalities to every child He sends into the world. Though it may take years to find out the qualities buried in every boy and girl, the search is worth every effort.

- **Encourage their desire to contribute.** Every child has a basic desire to be useful and constructive. Though this is part of every child's God-given nature, their better impulses are often offset by human weaknesses. Each one, therefore, needs encouragement and sympathetic guidance to lead a worthwhile life.

- **Help them to think and act for themselves.** The creative side of children is almost limitless. Avoid the danger of nipping in the bud a young person's natural instinct to be reasonably self-reliant. Too much independence too soon can hurt children. But it may be even more dangerous to regiment their every move.

Train children in the right way, and when old, they will not stray. (Proverbs 22:6)

Remind us, Lord, that You have given a distinct individuality to every child.

Entering the Christmas Story

Christmas is often described as a holiday for children, but really it's a "holy day" for people of all ages. Patheos writer Pat Gohn agrees, and shared some thoughts on how adults can better immerse themselves in the season's true meaning. She wrote:

"What if we prepared our hearts for Christmas not just by listening to or reading the Gospel, but by really entering into the story? Would God's story become ours?...It's a real spiritual exercise: a form of meditation that disallows just passively listening to the message, but actively receives it. Imagination stirs us to become a character in the story's action, or to see ourselves as bystanders or witnesses of the events...

"I discover that the supernatural takes place within the realm of my natural world. That's what makes Christmas so utterly amazing. My eyes see and my heart detects God becoming part of the human family, and I find Him in my own experiences...When my life glorifies and praises God for all I have heard and seen, then I am not only entering the story, I am living it."

The shepherds returned, glorifying and praising God for all they had heard and seen. (Luke 2:20)

Help me enter into Your presence, Jesus.

The Christmas Card Tree

At age five, Safyre Terry of Schenectady, New York, was burned on over 75 percent of her body in an arson-related fire that killed her father and siblings. How did she survive? Prayers and willpower, said her aunt Liz Dolder, who's now raising her.

Safyre, now age eight, has endured 65 surgeries and is scheduled for more. And yet, 2015 found her enjoying a Merry Christmas. Why?

The youngster asked Dolder to buy a Christmas tree on which she could hang cards from strangers. Dolder found one at Goodwill, then posted the request for cards on Facebook. She didn't expect much, but was surprised when 50 cards came in relatively fast. One said, "Dear Safyre, You deserve all the happiness in the world. Your outlook on life makes me smile, and your undefeatable attitude is what makes humans amazing."

Dolder told the *Washington Post,* "When you've seen the ugly in the world, and then you see the world come together for [Safyre], it's more than words can say. I'm so moved."

I cried to You for help, and You have healed me. (Psalm 30:2)

Remind me to bring joy to others this Christmas, Jesus.

The Queen's Christmas Message

Queen Elizabeth's 2015 Christmas message resonated with The Christophers. See if you can tell why from these excerpts: "For Joseph and Mary, the circumstances of Jesus's birth—in a stable—were far from ideal, but worse was to come as the family was forced to flee the country. It's no surprise that such a human story still captures our imagination and continues to inspire all of us who are Christians, the world over.

"Despite being displaced and persecuted throughout his short life, Christ's unchanging message was not one of revenge or violence but simply that we should love one another. Although it is not an easy message to follow, we shouldn't be discouraged; rather, it inspires us to try harder: to be thankful for the people who bring love and happiness into our own lives, and to look for ways of spreading that love to others...

"There's an old saying that 'it is better to light a candle than curse the darkness.' There are millions of people lighting candles of hope in our world today. Christmas is a good time to be thankful for them, and for all that brings light to our lives."

The light shines in the darkness, and the darkness did not overcome it. (John 1:5)

Guide me in adding my light and Yours to the world, Jesus.

The Kind of Greatness Christ Seeks

On her blog, Catholic author Danielle Bean recalled a favorite Christmas memory about Monsignor Leo, an elderly priest who served as pastor of a parish to which she belonged. He was especially popular with people at that time of year because he would always end his first Christmas mass by singing "O Holy Night" a cappella and without a microphone.

"Here was one man's simple expression of a great love he felt in his heart," wrote Bean. "Here was one man giving all of himself to God. God made him to sing, and so he sang. For God alone. With all that he had."

The simplicity of that expression of love resonated with Bean: "At Christmas, many of us feel pressured to do great things. We can't send out just *any* card; we can't give just *any* gift... Thankfully, the kind of greatness God asks of us is not as complicated as we sometimes make it ourselves. The kind of greatness God demands has nothing to do with ribbons or wrapping, packages or presents. The kind of greatness Christ seeks comes from small, ordinary things done with great love."

Anyone who loves God is known by Him. (1 Corinthians 8:3)

I devote my small acts of love to Your glory, Jesus.

The Best Christmas Gift Ever

"It was December 24, 1980, and the wait was grueling," recalls Tony Rossi, Director of Communications for The Christophers. "My 11-year-old self had asked for the popular 'large size Star Wars action figures' for Christmas, and I couldn't wait to find out whether they would be under the tree.

"But first came Christmas Eve vigil Mass with my mother, father, and maternal grandparents. Despite difficult challenges, like my grandfather's advancing Parkinson's Disease, we always went to church as a family. After Mass, we made the traditional rounds to my paternal grandparents, back to my maternal grandparents, and finally, home. Sure enough, Santa brought the action figures, and I thought it was the best Christmas gift ever.

"Adulthood brings a different perspective, though. While the toys provided me with hours of fun, it's the memories that I truly treasure because they were grounded in love. I was blessed to never lack love growing up, and I know now that gave me a great advantage in life. It is really those moments and memories that remain the best Christmas gifts I ever received."

Bless your Maker, who fills you with His good gifts. (Sirach 32:13)

Thank You for the gift of family, Jesus.

I Heard the Bells on Christmas Day

"I heard the bells on Christmas Day / Their old familiar carols play / And wild and sweet the words repeat / Of peace on earth, good-will to men."

Poet Henry Wadsworth Longfellow wrote those words in 1863, at a time when he especially needed the message of Christmas. His wife had passed away two years prior, and his son was wounded fighting for the North in the Civil War.

Despair worked its way into the poem, but so did hope, as other verses testify: "And in despair I bowed my head / 'There is no peace on earth,' I said / 'For hate is strong and mocks the song / Of peace on earth, good-will to men.'

"Then pealed the bells more loud and deep: / 'God is not dead, nor doth He sleep; / The wrong shall fail, the right prevail / With peace on earth, good-will to men.' / Till ringing singing, on its way / The world revolved from night to day / A voice, a chime, a chant sublime / Of peace on earth, good-will to men!"

In this world of strife and violence, be a messenger of peace on earth, good will to men.

Glory to God in the highest heaven, and on earth peace. (Luke 2:14)

Be my guide, infant Jesus, child of light.

God With Us

Today is the second day of the 12 days of Christmas, but instead of "two turtle doves," we'll give you this reflection from singer-songwriter Laura Story about the inspiration behind her Christmas album. During a "Christopher Closeup" interview, she explained, "The title 'God With Us' is more than a Christmas platitude. The fact that I have not walked through life alone has made all the difference.

"Even in the most lonely season, God has been with me because, 2,000 years ago, He saw how desperate humanity was and how in need we were of a savior. He sent Jesus not just to take away this problem of sin—even though that was His primary purpose—but so that we would never have to be alone again.

"I think about Christmas specifically. Some people think they're alone. And some people spend Christmas with family and friends, and still feel alone. So no matter what people are facing this holiday, I want them to remember that the Word truly did become flesh and dwelt among us so that we could feel His comfort and joy."

I am bringing you good news of great joy. (Luke 2:10)

Help me take comfort in You when I feel lonely, Jesus.

Admitting Mistakes

You may have heard of BBD&O, the legendary advertising agency. One of the founders, Bruce Barton, told this story about his working days as a young man.

He disagreed with his boss about something and offered facts to back up his opinion. His employer abruptly overruled him.

The next morning Barton got a call. "To my amazement, it was the boss. Said he: 'I have been thinking about our discussion of yesterday, and I just want you to know you were right and I was wrong.'"

Barton continued, "Years have gone by and I have known all sorts and conditions of men and women...They divide into two classes: those who feel they have lowered themselves by admitting a mistake, and so try in every way to rationalize it — and those who come out in forthright fashion and admit the facts."

Confess your sins to one another, and pray for one another, so that you may be healed. (James 5:16)

How liberating it is to be who I am: a person who can and does admit mistakes, Jesus.

Time For a Change?

If you're seriously considering eliminating an unwanted habit or establishing a new one, January 1st can seem a good time to start. But whether you're making a resolution for the new year or at another time, there are techniques people find helpful.

Nancy Bruning offers these tips in *Manhattan Times:*

- **Focus on actions, not outcomes.** Your goal might be to lose weight. But even if you don't drop the ideal 10 pounds, it can still be healthy to eat less and exercise more.

- **Take small steps.**

- **Establish new routines.** Replace an unwanted behavior with a positive habit.

- **Change your environment.** "I would light a cigarette every time the phone rang at one job. And when I quit [that job], I quit smoking."

- **Share your plans with others.** They will hold you accountable in friendly ways.

- **Don't let one slip-up derail you.** You *can* get back on track.

> **Let us consider how to provoke one another to love and good deeds. (Hebrews 10:24)**

> *Inspire us, Holy Spirit, to make changes that we know will improve our lives.*

From Clothes to Trash and Back Again

Ranya Kelly needed a box to ship some things, so she checked the trash bins behind a local mall. What she found was 500 pairs of shoes. Mrs. Kelly gathered the unused, discarded shoes and brought them to a shelter. That's how she began her commitment to get unsold clothes to people who don't have the means to buy them.

At first, stores were reluctant to help. "They were afraid people would try to return donated items for refunds," says the Arvada, Colorado homemaker. But now, a number of companies regularly supply shoes, clothing, blankets, and towels.

From their basement redistribution center, Kelly, her husband Byron and other volunteers send out over $2 million worth of donated merchandise. Shelters, hospitals, church groups and other agencies get the items to those who most need them.

You never know when some small event will change your life and the lives of others for the better—if you turn it into an opportunity to do good.

When you see the naked...cover them. (Isaiah 58:7)

Lord, let me be a useful tool of Your peace and comfort to anyone bruised by life.

A New Year's Eve to Remember

A New York City cop had come through for a tourist from Wisconsin on New Year's Eve. Now, this woman wanted nothing more than to return the favor—and so she did.

Diana Higgenbottom, 45, accompanied her husband Roger on a literal bucket-list trip. He had been diagnosed with cancer, and wanted to see the New Year's Eve Ball drop before he died. They had checked into a Times Square hotel, but then the news turned bad. Roger was desperately ill, and didn't know if he could make it. He decided to go at the last minute, but felt awful.

That's when New York cop Jamiel Altaheri—then a lieutenant—got involved. He had noticed the couple, seemingly in distress, found out their problem, and, with the help of other cops on the scene, ushered them to the best possible position—just in time to see the ball drop.

Roger died three months later, but Diana didn't forget Altaheri's kindness. She was there as a surprise guest when he was promoted to captain. He credits God with putting him in the right place at the right time—and Diana wholeheartedly agrees.

Who knows? Perhaps you have come to royal dignity for just such a time as this. (Esther 4:14)

God of kindness, place me where I may do the most good.

A Poem to Help You Meet Your Goals

American poet Edgar Guest held a particular grudge against the word "can't," as evidenced in these excerpts from one of his works (highlighted in the newsletter *Apple Seeds*):

"Can't is the worst word that's written or spoken;
Doing more harm here than slander and lies;
On it is many a strong spirit broken,
And with it many a good purpose dies...
Can't is the word that is foe to ambition,
An enemy ambushed to shatter your will;
Its prey is forever the man with a mission
And bows but to courage and patience and skill.
Hate it, with hatred that's deep and undying,
For once it is welcomed 'twill break any man;
Whatever the goal you are seeking, keep trying
And answer this demon by saying: 'I can.'"

Do not worry about anything, but in everything by prayer and supplication with thanksgiving let your requests be made known to God. (Philippians 4:6)

In times of doubt, Lord, fill me with Your everlasting hope and lead me toward achieving my goals.

Also Available

We hope that you have enjoyed *Three Minutes a Day, Volume 51.* These other Christopher offerings may interest you:

- **News Notes** are published 10 times a year on a variety of topics of current interest. Single copies are free; quantity orders available.

- **Appointment Calendars** are suitable for wall or desk and provide an inspirational message for each day of the year.

- **DVDs** include classic Christopher films, clay-animated Christmas stories, and Father John Catoir's reflections on making prayer simple and joyful.

- **Website—www.christophers.org**—has *Christopher Closeup* radio programs; links to our blog, Facebook and Twitter pages; a monthly *What's New* update; and much more.

For more information about The Christophers or to receive News Notes, please contact us:

The Christophers
5 Hanover Square
New York, NY 10004
Phone: 212-759-4050/888-298-4050
E-mail: mail@christophers.org
Website: www.christophers.org

The Christophers is a non-profit media organization founded in 1945 by Father James Keller, M.M. We share the message of personal responsibility and service to God and humanity with people of all faiths and no particular faith. Gifts are welcome and tax-deductible. Our legal title for wills is The Christophers, Inc.